Roger Moore's James Bond

- The Retrospective

John Fox

Contents

INTRODUCTION

According to Rotten Tomatoes, the worst three Bond films are
The Man with the Golden Gun, Octopussy, and A View To A
Kill. Here's the thing though. If I was at home for the night I'd
much rather watch any of these three films than No Time to
Die or Quantum of Solace. I'd also rather watch any of these
three films than Tomorrow Never Dies, The World Is Not
Enough or Die Another Day. Come to think of it I'd probably
rather watch The Man with the Golden Gun, Octopussy, or A
View To A Kill than Spectre or Skyfall too. Sure, Skyfall got
good reviews and is an interesting enough film but I know for
a fact that I'm definitely going to have way more fun watching
ANY Roger Moore film than Skyfall.

The era of James Bond under Roger Moore contains many of
my most golden and cherished Bond memories. The croc
escape in Live and Let Die, Bond's magnetic watch, the Lotus
chase in The Spy Who Loved Me, Richard Kiel as Jaws, the
freefall parachute jump in Moonraker, the Acrostar jet PTS in
Octopussy, Bond's fight on the train with Tee Hee - and so on.
And yet, I am constantly encountering modern articles about
how terrible Roger Moore and his Bond films were! How can
an era which contains many of my most indelible Bond
memories be terrible? The Roger Moore era was never terrible.
The Roger Moore era was fantastic. It was fun.

Back in the early 1970s there was considerable doubt that the
Bond franchise had any sort of future without Sean Connery. It
was only expected to wheeze on for a couple more films after
Connery departed (again) in the wake of Diamonds Are
Forever. At this tricky time, Roger Moore was cast as James
Bond in 1972. He was 45 years old and had just made the
lightweight but diverting television show The Persuaders with
Tony Curtis. Roger later confessed that even he thought the
Bond goose was cooked. He felt it was unlikely that he would
actually get to make the three films he was now under contract
to appear in.

However, this did not turn out to be the case at all. Roger Moore did something that was hitherto regarded to be nigh on impossible. He proved that the Bond franchise could survive, flourish even, way beyond Sean Connery. For new generations of Bond fans Roger Moore became the Bond they grew up with. Roger made seven films and ensured that the series would survive way beyond the 1970s. That is a remarkable feat for any actor isn't it? Roger, who was always so unfairly derided as an actor, had sufficient screen presence, charisma, wit, and intelligence to put his own personal stamp on James Bond and move it ever so slightly out of Sean Connery's mighty shadow. Roger made the character his own by doing it his way.

And yet, if you glance at lazy modern casual Bond retrospectives, Roger rarely seems to get any respect at all. Many of his films seem to end up at the bottom of subjective Bond ranking lists and Roger is too often casually dismissed as some geriatric comedian who blighted the Bond franchise and turned it into something akin to the Carry On series. Now, I would concede that Roger probably made one or two films too many and I can understand why his Bond wouldn't be everyone's cup of tea (in the same way that, for different reasons, Timothy Dalton and Daniel Craig aren't everyone's cup of tea) but I can't help feeling that Roger's era, which was often highly entertaining and lavish, is sorely and unfairly underrated by this casual disdain.

If you watch Live and Let Die, Roger Moore is arguably the most youthful of the Bond actors. He is positively boyish in that film! Roger in The Spy Who Loved Me is for me one of the great Bond performances by any actor. Roger looks fantastic in that film and his ability to remain a witty and commanding anchor for a picture that big and that crazy is a testament to his screen presence. Granted, the comedic elements in Roger's films got out of hand at times but notice how good he is whenever he is given a 'straight' scene to play. The moment where Bond emerges from the out of control centrifuge in Moonraker, all sweaty and rattled and unable to talk, is a great piece of acting. Despite all the self-deprecation and brickbats, Roger was always much better than either he or critics gave him any credit for.

The Bond franchise is elastic enough to encompass different interpretations and as such I think Roger's lighter take on Bond in the 1970s was perfectly valid, enjoyable, and in many cases iconic. Roger's era had John Barry, Ken Adam, Lewis Gilbert, Derek Meddings, Richard Maibum, Tom Mankiewicz, Maurice Binder, and Cubby Broccoli. In retrospect it was something of a golden era for Bond. The success of The Spy Who Loved Me and Moonraker was almost a throwback to the gilt edged Bondmania of Connery and the 1960s.

One could argue that, in light of his age, Roger might have been best served being the 'seventies Bond' and making way for a Lewis Collins, Timothy Dalton, or Michael Billington at the dawn of the 1980s but the reason they kept bringing Roger back was because he was established as Bond and also popular with audiences. If people hadn't enjoyed Roger's Bond they wouldn't have made seven films with him! If he was even half as bad as these modern commentators make out then Roger would have been dumped long before 1985.

In the book that follows we shall take a deep dive into the Roger Moore era of Bond and explore his tenure from start to finish. We'll assess the strengths and weaknesses of both Roger's Bond and his films but most of all this book is a celebration of Roger Moore's James Bond and the years he spent suavely karate chopping baddies in a selection of safari suits and cream flares. Roger's amazing contribution to the Bond franchise is far too often derided and mocked these days. This book will hopefully serve as an entertaining and robust defence of Roger and his incarnation of James Bond.

CHAPTER ONE - BEFORE BOND

Roger George Moore was born on the 14th of October 1927 in Stockwell, London. Despite his urbane image as the archetypal English gentleman, Moore came from a fairly humble background and was a policeman's son from South London. He lived through some of the Luftwaffe's London Blitz before evacuation to Devon, did national military service (where he eventually earned the rank of captain), and had early ambitions to become an animator. It was of course though acting which became his career. Roger eventually went to Rada where he met Lois Maxwell, who was later to play Miss Moneypenny in the Connery and Moore Bond films.

Like any jobbing young actor, Roger Moore experienced provincial theatres and tatty boarding houses as he sought to carve out a career. His good looks eventually earned him a contract with MGM - though big screen stardom was still elusive for a long time. He was married to the singer Dorothy Squires (who was rather eccentric it seems) for a time and appeared on the screen with some very famous faces. Roger's early roles included uncredited parts in films and some small roles in television shows and television movies. He made his film debut in the 1954 film The Last Time I Saw Paris. The Last Time I Saw Paris was based on the F Scott Fitzgerald short story Babylon Revisited. Despite his studio contract, MGM seemed to show little interest in activating their option on Roger until this film arrived.

Roger was asked to report to Culver City Studios in Hollywood where the Irving Thalberg building dominated the landscape. Roger Moore was 26 years-old and awed by the studio with its collection of lots - all with spectacular backdrops to use in films. New York City streets, railway tracks, cowboy towns, lakes, rivers. The stars of The Last Time I Saw Paris were Elizabeth Taylor and Van Johnson with Roger some way down the cast list as a minor supporting player. The talented director Richard Brooks would further enhance his reputation with films like Blackboard Jungle, Cat on a Hot Tin Roof, and

Elmer Gantry. Roger - looking incredibly young - flits into the film as a tennis playing gigolo who has a fling with Helen and makes Van Johnson jealous. Roger doesn't have an awful lot to do in the film but you can see why his good looks encouraged studios to have him on a contract just in case they needed a dashing young actor for any particular part.

In 1955, Roger appeared in a supporting role in Interrupted Melody - a biopic of Australian opera singer Marjorie Lawrence. Lawrence valiantly battled polio after huge success in the 1930s and the film is an adaptation of her book about her ups and downs and experiences around the world as a famed singer. Lana Turner, Greer Garson, and Kathryn Grayson were considered to play Lawrence but it was Eleanor Parker who won the role. Glenn Ford was cast as Marjorie's doctor husband Thomas King while Roger plays her brother Cyril. The voice of Lawrence singing was supplied by Eileen Farrell. Interrupted Melody is regarded to be a fine biopic of the era and arguably the highlight of Eleanor Parker's career.

1955 also saw Roger appear in The King's Thief. The King's Thief is a Hollywood swashbuckler with many British actors in the cast. The film was roasted by critics and isn't fondly remembered (even Roger jokes about how awful the film was in his autobiography) but the picture was important to Roger on a personal note because he became great friends with David Niven through it. The production was notable for some behind the scenes intrigue with Edmund Purdom frequently holding everyone up with constant telephone calls due to his affair with Linda Christian. Another British cast member, George Sanders, was prone to falling asleep in his dressing room. It's a wonder the film was ever finished!

The following year Roger Moore appeared in another movie - Diane. Diane is a historical drama about the life of Diane de Poitiers. Diane de Poitiers was a noblewoman and courtier at the courts of kings Francis I and his son - Henry II. She became notorious as the latter's favourite and developed much influence and power at the French Court. The leading lady in

Diane was Lana Turner, a huge Hollywood star but now slightly on the downward slope. It was the last film of Turner's MGM contract.

Diane was also Roger's final film as part of his MGM contract and he takes on the part of Prince Henri. Co-star Pedro Armendáriz would go on to become well known to James Bond fans for his role as Kerim Bey in From Russia with Love with Sean Connery. Diane was not a huge financial success but the production values of the film were praised and it served as a respectable last hurrah for Lana Turner's MGM years. Roger is very dashing and handsome as Henri - although he doesn't seem completely comfortable in period clobber. He and Turner work together relatively well and do their best to stir some passion into the picture. The age difference between the characters is less of a factor in this interpretation but Roger does look very baby-faced and young compared to the statuesque Turner.

In 1958/59, Roger appeared in 39 episodes as the lead of the ITV show Ivanhoe. Big screen stardom might have thus far eluded Roger but he was a great leading man on television and good at playing heroic and dashing heroes. One of his Ivanhoe co-stars was Robert Brown - who many years later would play M in his last Bond movies. Ivanhoe was the first time Roger had been a leading man in anything. He did many of his own stunts in Ivanhoe and picked up a number of injuries as a result. The show was made by ITV and aimed primarily at children.

Roger Moore's flexibility, in that he was willing to work in either film or television and on both sides of the Atlantic too, meant that he was never short of work. In 1959/1960, Roger appeared in 37 episodes of the Western television show The Alaskans and also found the time to appear in the anthology show Alfred Hitchcock Presents. The Alaskans was Roger's first experience of American television and he absolutely hated it. Roger described the show as 'appalling' and felt that the actors were frequently placed in unnecessary danger with the stunts, fires, and (a particular bugbear) fake plastic snow. Roger's marriage was also strained by him having an affair with his Alaskans co-star Dorothy Provine. It's safe to say that The Alaskans was not an especially happy time for Roger.

Roger, much to his annoyance, also appeared in the fourth season of the Western show Maverick as Beau Maverick. Roger replaced James Garner - who quit the show over a contract dispute. Roger was told he was going to be in Maverick while he was in the make-up chair on The Alaskans. He was irritated by this because he had some film offers in the pipeline and felt the writing on Maverick was atrocious. Roger made fourteen episodes of Maverick before he decided he'd had enough and quit. Sean Connery actually turned down the part of Beau Maverick before it was given to Roger Moore. Connery and Moore would forever be entwined in cinema history thanks to an altogether different role in the future.

Roger also appeared in the 1959 film The Miracle. The film is adapted from The Miracle (1911) by German playwright Karl Vollmoeller. Volmoeller based the play on a Middle Ages legend of a Virgin Mary statue replacing a nun who flees a convent with a knight. The film was supposed to be made in the 1940s but was long delayed and only arrived in 1959.

The story here moves the legend to the Napoleonic era and has Carroll Baker as the lead. Baker, a famous sex symbol of the era, (unwittingly) created controversy in Elia Kazan's suggestive Baby Doll a few years before. It was speculated that her playing a postulant in a convent in a moral message film was an attempt to quash the controversy that still lingered from censorious religious groups! She simply didn't want to be typecast.

The Miracle was intended as a Bette Davis vehicle but she wasn't interested. Roger's part as a British officer was initially offered to Dirk Bogarde but he wasn't interested either. Bogarde suggested to the studio that Roger play the role instead. When Roger later tried to personally thank Dirk

Bogarde for suggesting him he found it completely impossible to get a meeting with the reclusive actor! The Miracle met with a tepid reception both from audiences and critics. It wasn't helped by opening against Ben-Hur and also suffered in comparison to Audrey Hepburn's The Nun's Story.

Roger would appear in three more films in the early 1960s before taking a long hiatus from movies thanks to his role as Simon Templar in The Saint on television. The Sins of Rachel Cade was part of Roger's contract with Warner's and saw him appear with Angie Dickinson and Peter Finch. Roger was still shooting the television show The Alaskans and only arrived on the set of The Sins of Rachel Cade as Finch was preparing to leave so they didn't spend much time together. Roger's friend Gordon Douglas directed the picture. The Sins of Rachel Cade is a so-so melodrama that is competent enough but perhaps not the most memorable of the early films that Roger acted in.

The Sins of Rachel Cade is a very late fifties/early sixties soap opera-ish drama with the Belgian Congo quite obviously a few sets out the back of the Warner's lot rather than a real jungle. Some stock footage from The Nun's Story was also used in the film. The same year Roger also appeared in Gold of the Seven Saints. Gold of the Seven Saints is a Western that features Roger alongside the brawny Clint Walker. The director Gordon Douglas and Walker had already made 1958's Fort Dobbs and 1959's Yellowstone Kelly together and Gold of the Seven Saints was their final Western collaboration. Walker is the lead and Gold of the Seven Saints feels like an attempt to make the hulking actor (then appearing in the popular television series Cheyenne) and Roger stars on the big screen.

One could forgive Roger if he was starting to tire of Westerns somewhat after his television experiences but Gold of the Seven Saints turned out to be a decent enough picture. Gold of the Seven Saints is sometimes dubbed an inferior The Treasure of the Sierra Madre and while, yes, it's true that Sierra Madre is a much better film, Gold of the Seven Saints is an interesting and well made picture with some beautiful black and white photography by Joseph F Biroc.

The final film role Roger took at this was time was Romulus and the Sabines. Romulus and the Sabines (Il ratto delle sabine) is an Italian/French swords and sandals picture directed by Richard Pottier. A film inspired by the mythological Rape of the Sabine Women. Roger was persuaded to participate by his agent at the time - despite the fee on offer seeming rather modest. Appearing in European films was seen as a way to boost one's profile and stay busy. It certainly worked for Clint Eastwood.

Romulus and the Sabines was not a huge success though and has largely been forgotten today. It was a cheapjack production with not much money to go around. Roger was supposed to make another Italian picture after this but he had so much trouble getting his money for Romulus and the Sabines he decided not to bother. In his memoir, Roger reflects that it was an interesting experience making the film, especially as the actors spoke in their native languages and were simply dubbed afterwards.

In 1961, Roger was cast by Lew Grade as Simon Templar in a new adaptation of The Saint, based on the novels by Leslie Charteris. Moore played the debonair troubleshooter Simon Templar and often directed the episodes too. Roger would play this role for seven years. NBC picked up The Saint and so the show, much more than any of the movies Roger had been in, made him something of an international star. Roger never really escaped from the suave eyebrow raised image of Simon Templar - though this didn't unduly bother him.

In his memoir, Roger Moore recalls cold winter days in Elstree shooting The Saint and always having to pretend on minimal budgets that Templar was in some exotic land far away. Roger was suave and handsome as Templar and convincing as an aristocratic hero who is very sure of himself. Templar had fistfights, romanced women, and drove posh cars. Simon Templar was a lot like James Bond in many ways so it probably wasn't surprising that Roger was touted as a potential James Bond quite a lot in the 1960s when the 007 franchise was born. Going from Templar to Bond felt like a fairly natural progression.

The first screen adaptation of James Bond was a 1954 CBS version of Casino Royale as part of Climax Mystery Theater. Barry Nelson portrayed 'Jimmy' Bond - an American card shark. This one hour production obviously wasn't tremendously faithful to Ian Fleming. Bond eventually managed to escape from such curiosities and become a juggernaut movie franchise on the silver screen. The James Bond film franchise (based of course on the popular series of spy thrillers written by Ian Fleming) launched in 1962 is a very special and unique series quite unlike any other. When it began no one could have possibly dreamed of the success and longevity it would enjoy. There had been franchises before Bond - like Tarzan, Sherlock Holmes, Charlie Chan, The Falcon, Jungle Jim, Frankenstein, Lassie, Rin Tin Tin, Bulldog Drummond, Hopalong Cassidy, and many others. As the Bond series began, thrifty but fun franchises like Godzilla and the Carry On films were already becoming popular in their respective countries.

The Bond franchise created by producers Cubby Broccoli and Harry Saltzman however was completely different. Previous film series operated strictly on the law of diminishing returns and lowered the budgets accordingly. They sought to extract every last penny out of their licenced property without actually spending any money. The Bond series reversed this tradition. Each new Bond film was bigger than the one that came before. More lavish, more expensive, more spectacular. It was a gamble that paid off handsomely. Adjusted for inflation, the most successful James Bond film of all time is 1965's Thunderball. Thunderball marked the peak of sixties Bondmania but the series would still go on and on with enduring success and seemingly without end.

The James Bond books were turned into a movie franchise in

1962 by New York born film producer Albert 'Cubby' Broccoli and Canadian producer Harry Saltzman. Before he became a film producer, Cubby Broccoli had a spell selling coffins. He was also a Christmas tree salesman at one point. Dr No was eventually chosen to be the first film adaptation.

"Harry Saltzman held the option on Ian Fleming's James Bond stories," said Broccoli, "and I offered him a partnership. He considered them a bit of nonsense. I thought they offered all the basics in screen entertainment: a virile and resourceful hero, exotic locations, the ingenious apparatus of espionage and sex on a sophisticated level. It's true they had been around for a long time, and none of the leading British and American producers had made a serious pitch for them."

Cubby Broccoli used to be a business partner with the famous American producer Irwin Allen. When Cubby told Allen he wanted to option the Bond books, Allen told him the Fleming novels were awful and wouldn't even be worthy of television. He was obviously completely wrong about that. Ian Fleming's James Bond books were very popular because their blend of sex, sadism, and dangerous adventure felt like something new and even risque at the time. British readers loved the James Bond books in the 1950s because the exotic nature of the novels was an escape from the lingering post-war austerity they still experienced.

Fleming once wrote that the James Bond books were written for 'for warm-blooded heterosexuals in railway trains, airplanes and beds'. Bond's code number '007' was apparently inspired by a bus route in Kent which was often taken by the author Ian Fleming. The literary Bond suffers from "accidie" - this is Fleming's definition of boredom and the deadliest of all sins for James Bond. The profile of the Bond novels got a huge boost when President John F. Kennedy named From Russia With Love as one of his books of the year.

As part of the deal with Ian Fleming to bring James Bond to the big screen, it was agreed that EON (the company created by Broccoli and Saltzman to produce the movies - EON means Everything or Nothing) would have permission to write original Bond films if they exhausted the Fleming stories. This was obviously a shrewd agreement on the part of the film producers. When the Bond movie franchise began, Ian Fleming was allowed to sit in on production meetings and had final script approval. The James Bond movie franchise tended to cherrypick titles, character names, and scenes from the Fleming books rather than adapt them wholesale.

Broccoli and Saltzman finally managed to put in a deal in place for the first Bond movie to be produced but now they had the not inconsiderable task of finding the right actor to play Bond. This would be their first experience of what you might describe as the 007 casting circus. The casting of a new Bond involves hundreds of interviews, readings, auditions, and screen tests. There is no particular science about it. The process simply has to find an actor who everyone (the producers and the studio) can agree upon. The lack of a specific criteria for what sort of person they wanted was evident in the eclectic sweep of the Dr No casting calls. Mature and famous actors were approached to play James Bond in Dr No but so were inexperienced unknown young actors too. No one really seemed to have a firm idea of who they wanted.

When the first James Bond film was being planned, Ian Fleming sent Broccoli and Saltzman a memo with his own thoughts about the approach they should take. 'Atmosphere: To my mind, the greatest danger in this series is too much stage Englishness,' wrote Fleming. 'There should, I think, be no monocles, mustaches, bowler hats or bobbies or other "Limey" gimmicks. There should be no blatant English slang, a minimum of public school ties and accents.' Fleming wanted the Bond films to feel modern and bold. Broccoli and Saltzman shared this vision. Cubby Broccoli's own take was that Bond films should be set 'five minutes into the future'. They should exist in a world that is more or less our own but heightened slightly.

It is often said that Ian Fleming wanted Roger Moore to play
James Bond in Dr No but any evidence for this is hard to
verify. Moore said that he wasn't approached for Dr No at all -
although Cubby Broccoli wrote in his memoir that Roger was a
person they briefly discussed in casting discussions but then
dismissed because they felt he still looked too boyish and
callow. At the time Roger Moore was in his early thirties and
on the lower rung of the studio system in Hollywood. Roger's
attempt to become a star in the United States, despite frequent
work, did not gain much traction and so he eventually
returned to England to play Simon Templar on television -
thus setting him on a 'long way around' path to James Bond in
the future.

The problems in casting James Bond in Dr No felt like divine
intervention in the end because it paved the way for the right
candidate to finally emerge. That candidate was a 30 year-old
Scottish actor named Sean Connery. Connery had been an
artist's model, body builder, and coffin polisher before he took
up acting. It was apparently the 1959 Disney film Darby O'Gill
and the Little People which put Connery on the EON radar.
Cubby Broccoli's wife Dana saw Connery in this film and told
her husband that Connery was sexy. When the producers met
Sean Connery they were impressed by the macho magnetism
he seemed to project.

'One face kept coming back into my mind,' wrote Cubby
Broccoli in his memoir. 'He was Sean Connery, a tall,
personable man, projecting a kind of animal virility and just
the right hint of threat behind that hard smile. I was convinced
he was the closest we could get to Fleming's super-hero. We
sent footage to United Artists in New York, who'd put up the
$1 million. They sent back a telegram: 'NO – KEEP TRYING.'
We wired back, insisting that Connery was the man we wanted
and we weren't searching any further.'

Connery was scruffy and laid-back when he met the producers.
He wasn't someone to put on heirs and graces. "I had first met
Sean in Cubby's office back at the beginning," said

Moneypenny actress Lois Maxwell. "He had that wonderful atmosphere of menace and moved, as Cubby said, like a panther. But he was still a poor young actor in rumpled corduroys who looked like he lived in a bedsit." Connery was even reluctant to do a test for Bond. He said the producers should simply decide if they wanted him or not on the strength of his other work (which was limited at the time as Connery had only been acting for several years).

Terence Young hated the choice of Sean Connery at first ("Disaster!" Young is said to have declared when he heard Connery was cast) but quickly realised that Connery could be very good if he was cleaned up somewhat. Terence Young played a big role in the transformation of Connery. Young had his tailor cut sharp suits for Connery and taught him how to be more elegant and refined onscreen. Young got Sean Connery a Saville Row suit for Dr No and told him to sleep in it! Young wanted Connery to feel like an expensive suit was like a second skin. The friendship between Terence Young and Sean Connery on the early Bond films mitigated the fact that Connery didn't like the Bond producers very much. When he was cast as James Bond, Connery worked with a dance teacher named Yat Malmgren so he could learn how to be more graceful and panther like in his movements and gestures.

Ian Fleming also initially hated the choice of Sean Connery to play James Bond. Fleming thought that Connery was too rough and not refined enough to play his hero. He even compared him to a truck driver. However, Fleming changed his mind when he saw Connery in action. He thought Connery was fantastic. Ian Fleming lived long enough to see Dr No and From Russia With Love made into movies but - sadly - he died just before the release of Goldfinger. Fleming therefore never quite got to experience the peak Bondmania that his famous character created in the 1960s with Goldfinger and Thunderball. Peter Hunt, the editor on the early Bond films, said they only realised what a sensation they had on their hands when they screened Dr No for an audience. Before that, they genuinely didn't know if audiences would like Dr No or not.

Sean Connery said he enjoyed making the first few Bond films but it became a drag in the end. "The first two or three were fun. The cast made it fun. Jumping out of planes was entertaining although it was tough on my hair piece. It eventually became too dominant in everything I was doing. There was no way to compete with it and try to get any justifiable balance." The Bond films soon got bigger and bigger as the money rolled in. Thunderball was so popular in Britain that some cinemas sold all their seats and then sold extra tickets to customers who were willing to stand! Demand for Thunderball was so great that they had two simultaneous premieres in London full of celebrities, glitz, and huge crowds of fans. Sean Connery never turned up to either of them.

All of the later James Bond actors have had to stand in the shadow cast by the Sean Connery. George Lazenby once said that the post-Connery Bonds were essentially all impostors trying to play a role that belonged to Sean. Connery had screen presence, charisma, perfect timing, machismo, acting ability, and wit. He was the complete package. None of the other Bond actors (whatever their individual strengths) were quite able to tick every box in the way that Sean Connery did (and with considerable ease too). Connery's Bond could be cruel and ruthless but he was also charming and funny. No other Bond actor was able to project an irresistible blend of power and panache in the fashion that Connery could. Connery's Bond was dangerous but he was also fun. That was the perfect template for the cinematic version of Ian Fleming's character.

Sean Connery has to take a generous portion of the credit for the Bond films becoming such a phenomenon that they still exist today. The 60s Bonds were the foundation upon which an apparently indestructible film franchise was built. Dr No made nearly $60 million from a budget of only one million and the profits on the following films would be even more spectacular. Goldfinger was so popular that its soundtrack knocked the Beatles off the top of the American albums chart. Production began on Goldfinger before From Russia with Love had even been released to cinemas. The producers were super confident (even at this early stage) that they had a winning formula.

In 1964, Roger Moore unofficially played James Bond for the first time in a sketch on the comedy show Mainly Millicent with Millicent Martin. The sketch was obviously played for laughs but it indicated how Roger was already being associated with James Bond in the eyes of the public and media. Because of his suave hero image as Simon Templar, people were already speculating about the possibility of Roger taking over as James Bond should Sean Connery ever decide to depart for pastures new.

Sean Connery would make five Bond films in the 1960s. It was as if the union of this actor and this character was always destined to happen. You couldn't really imagine anyone else playing the sixties Bond. Connery was perfect. Though the role catapulted Connery to the A' list it did not bring him artistic happiness. Sean Connery quickly tired of the fame and attention afforded to him by Bondmania in the 1960s. Connery called James Bond his Frankenstein's Monster. In the period between Thunderball and You Only Live Twice, Connery did an interview in which he said - "The Bond pictures have become like comic strips dependent on bigger and better gimmicks. That's all that sustains them. There are even dolls with spikes that protrude from their shoes. It's a lot of rubbish."

One of the main reasons why Connery left the franchise was that he felt it was constrictive playing the same character all the time. He wanted to embrace new challenges as an actor and get away from his Bond image. Connery was frustrated that the Bond films became increasingly elaborate and lengthy productions because this made it more difficult for him to find the time to play other more rewarding (from his point of view) roles. There are other reasons too why Sean Connery tired of playing James Bond. For one, he felt like he had no privacy anymore. Wherever he went he was besieged by fans. Connery couldn't even go out for a quiet meal without being asked for an autograph (his annoyance was frequently made worse by people asking him to sign autographs 'James Bond' rather than Sean Connery). Around the time that Thunderball was released, Sean Connery received about 1,500 fan letters a week.

Another big reason why Connery became embittered was money. Broccoli and Saltzman were raking it in with the Bond franchise in the 1960s and Connery felt he should have been made a partner and given a more generous share of the profits. "It's not that I needed the money," said Connery in 1971, "I'm a relatively wealthy man. It was the fact that I put in an awful lot of work and energy into the Bond pictures and was not sufficiently rewarded. The producers were getting greedy. I had an awful time getting the money out of them." Broccoli and Saltzman, in response, might have argued that they were the ones who made Connery a film star in the first place. Sean Connery would have been nowhere near as rich and famous as he was without James Bond.

Before the drama of casting 007 in On Her Majesty's Secret Service began, Roger Moore had a vague approach to play James Bond in the late 1960s. Cubby and Harry were thinking about making The Man with the Golden Gun at the time and thought Roger (now popular and famous thanks to the television show The Saint) might be a safe pair of hands for the franchise. Roger was a neighbour of Harry Saltzman in the 1960s and knew both Cubby and Harry quite well. "At that time they were talking about going to Cambodia," said Roger, "and all hell broke loose and things got postponed. Lew Grade decided to sell a series Tony Curtis and I were doing - The Persuaders - which sort of precluded me from doing Bond. Then they had the search and came up with George Lazenby."

George Lazenby was cast as James Bond only weeks before On Her Majesty's Secret Service began production. When Lazenby replaced Sean Connery as Bond, they were originally going to say that Bond had plastic surgery to fool his enemies as a means to explain why James Bond didn't look like Sean Connery anymore! However, this idea was sensibly abandoned in the end. Audiences were well aware that the actor had changed. When Lazenby turned up to Pinewood Studios for the first day of shooting a security guard failed to recognize him and wouldn't let him in. That was more or less Lazenby's Bond career in a nutshell. He was the 'other fella' sandwiched between the large shadows cast by Sean Connery and Roger Moore.

On Her Majesty's Secret Service, the first Bond film not to feature Sean Connery, is often written about as if it was a dreadful failure but this was not the case. Sure, audiences at the time unavoidably missed Sean Connery but the film made some money and is now felt by many fans (and I would include myself among them) to be the best James Bond movie ever made. It should be noted that Connery probably wouldn't have mustered much enthusiasm for OHMSS even if he had somehow been lured back. Besides, one of the strengths of the film was that Lazenby's youth and inexperience gave him a vulnerability which wouldn't have been so believable if conveyed by Connery's Bond. Oddly enough, Lazenby, though an inferior actor, actually suited the more human story of OHMSS more than Connery.

Strangely, it's not that difficult to watch OHMSS and just accept this is still Connery's Bond only with a different actor - and the film is determined to run with that concept, even linking the title sequence into the Connery films. Lazenby was chosen because of his physical similarities to Connery. As with Connery, Lazenby was also believably tough and had a rough and ready sort of quality. After George Lazenby declined an invitation to return as James Bond in Diamonds Are Forever, he was frozen as the 'one-off Bond' and it was often wrongly assumed that both Lazenby and OHMSS had been a failure. Over time though, the strengths of the film have been rightly acknowledged.

After the end of his popular television series The Saint, Roger was approached by United Artists with the offer of a three film deal. He was keen to get back into making films after years on the small screen as Simon Templar and an action comedy espionage caper called Crossplot was the result. Leigh Vance and John Kruse, two writers from The Saint, were brought in to write the screenplay and Roger took the lead role as Gary Fenn, an advertising executive who ends up in a John Buchanite adventure. The film was not a success though and the two other proposed pictures for United Artists were quietly shelved - although Roger and Robert S Baker's production company did go on to make The Man Who Haunted Himself.

In his memoir Roger suggested that Crossplot was rushed into production too soon without the nuts and bolts of the screenplay being in place. Production on The Saint had only finished a month before so one can see how difficult it must have been to make Crossplot with so little preparation. Crossplot is often described as a 'dry run' for Roger Moore at James Bond four years before he played 007 for the first time in Live and Let Die. One can see elements in this although Crossplot seems more influenced at times by Hitchcockian thrillers like North By Northwest. Imagine Hitchcock, The Saint, James Bond, and a Swinging Sixties comedy caper all blended together and you aren't a million light years away from Crossplot even if the end product is frustratingly less than the sum of its parts.

In 1970, Roger made what is probably his best film outside of the Bond franchise with The Man Who Haunted Himself. The Man Who Haunted Himself is a cult 1970 British film directed by Basil Dearden and based on the novel The Strange Case of Mr Pelham by Anthony Armstrong and an episode of Alfred Hitchcock Presents that previously adapted the story. The film is an intriguing and overlooked psychological thriller with a supernatural atmosphere and stars Roger as a successful but uptight and work obsessed businessman called Harold Pelham.

Driving home from his job in the city one afternoon, Pelham

has a very bad car accident that leaves him fighting for his life and a strange incident duly occurs in the hospital. Pelham is declared momentarily dead and two hearts briefly flicker on his monitor but he recovers and returns home, eventually resuming his job again after a short break abroad. Back at work though, some very odd things soon start to occur in Harold's life. Colleagues keep mentioning meetings or conversations they've had with him that Pelham has no memory of whatsoever and he is even told he's apparently agreed to a merger of the company despite being adamant he made no such decision.

Pelham is more perplexed than ever when informed he was clearly seen playing billiards in London on a day when he knows for a fact he was recuperating in Spain. As these incidents escalate it almost appears to Pelham that he has a strange double or impostor who always seems to be one step ahead of him and who somehow represents the more wild and suppressed nature of his personality - causing all manner of mayhem to his own life. Is Pelham going mad? The victim of an elaborate practical joke? Or does he really have a malevolent doppelganger attempting to take over his life?

Roger Moore took a smaller than usual fee to help get The Man Who Haunted Himself made and while it wasn't a success at the time (the actor blamed the poor marketing) it is now regarded to be something of a cult favourite and the best picture Roger made outside of the James Bond series. Roger cited The Man Who Haunted Himself as his favourite film out of those he made. The Man Who Haunted Himself is undoubtedly Roger Moore's finest hour outside of his long stint in the tuxedo and safari suit as James Bond and this likable and absorbing Twilight Zone style mystery shows that the oft-maligned and rather self-deprecating star was in reality always a lot better than he or anyone else ever gave him credit for when actually required to do some acting. He gives a surprisingly skillful and natural performance here as the increasingly confused and rattled Pelham and makes the plight of the central character both believable and moving at times.

Meanwhile, the Bond producers and United Artists now faced their ultimate nightmare after OHMSS. They had to find a new James Bond actor much sooner than expected for the next picture - Diamonds Are Forever. It must have felt like the dust had only just settled on the endless interviews, readings, and auditions for OHMSS but now they had to do it all over again! One name who again couldn't be considered was Roger Moore. Moore began shooting the television show The Persuaders with Tony Curtis in 1970 and was unavailable. The Persuaders was likeable fluff which had Moore and Curtis playing playboy troubleshooters (one an English toff and the other a self-made millionaire from New York - you can probably guess who played who!) who swan around various exotic locations. The Persuaders benefited greatly from the fact that Moore and Curtis clearly liked each other and so had good comic chemistry.

For a brief moment in time, John Gavin was officially signed on the dotted line to play James Bond in Diamonds Are Forever. Gavin was forty years-old and certainly looked the part. He was handsome, dark-haired, and muscular. Gavin made his film debut in 1956 and was probably best known for playing Sam Loomis in Hitchcock's Psycho. Gavin had also played Julius Caesar in Kubrick's Spartacus and appeared in Thoroughly Modern Millie with Julie Andrews. What probably landed Gavin the Bond role was the 1968 film OSS 117 – Double Agent. OSS 117 – Double Agent was what you might describe as a Spaghetti spy film and one of the many European James Bond mimics or parodies that festooned the 1960s.

OSS 117 is Hubert Bonisseur de La Bath, a fictional secret agent created by French writer Jean Bruce. A number of actors have played this character in tongue-in-cheek and Bondish parodies. The producers clearly watched Gavin in this spy spoof and thought he would make a passable Bond. The signing of Gavin was a surprise mainly because he was American. Gavin was also no Laurence Olivier and his signing seemed somewhat of an act of desperation - as if EON were struggling to find an actor so just picked the most James

Bondish looking person they could find and didn't worry about whether he could act or not. "Time was getting awfully short", said Cubby Broccoli. "We had to have someone in the bullpen."

United Artists were not enthused at all by the selection of John Gavin. They saw Gavin as an actor who was on the slide as his recent projects had included a failed television Western film pitched as a pilot for a proposed show and a supporting role in the megabomb comedy Pussycat, Pussycat, I Love You. The studio, still bruised by the Lazenby affair, wanted someone more famous than John Gavin to play Bond. United Artists decided that the only thing to do was to get Sean Connery back - at any cost. This required the studio to pay a then unheard of fee amounting to $1.25 million (which Connery donated to charity), finance two film projects of Connery's choice, and also pay the actor compensation for any overrun in the weekly shooting schedule.

It was a sensational deal at the time and illustrated that as far as United Artists were concerned the Bond franchise was simply not viable without Sean Connery. The unlucky John Gavin was compensated financially by the studio for the termination of his contract and drifted into television roles. In 1981 he became the United States Ambassador to Mexico. "It was a business agreement—with our consent of course," said Cubby Broccoli of removing Gavin as Bond to make way for Connery. "So we accepted that fact that Sean is Bond—but not that John is not. I think John Gavin will be eligible for the James Bond role when it comes up again."

Diamonds Are Forever saw a big lurch in tone towards tongue-in-cheek humour after the more sombre and tragic events of On Her Majesty's Secret Service. While purists might have been dismayed by this shift to a more campy and flippant type of Bond film, from a commercial point of view it made sense and the flaws in the movie were mitigated by the delight audiences felt at Sean Connery's return. The plot of Diamonds Are Forever is vague to the extreme and some of the special effects are strangely mediocre for a James Bond production (the satellite set-piece is atrocious) but the feeling of aimlessness that seems to dog Diamonds Are Forever is compensated for by some fun escapism - like the oil pipe sequence, Bond's fight in the elevator, the Las Vegas car stunt (where the Mustang famously comes out of the alleyway the wrong way up), and the large scale oil rig battle sequence at the end.

A 40 year-old Sean Connery is clearly coasting in Diamonds are Forever. He's a little bit pudgy and has the air of a man who is slightly impatient to get back to the golf course. However, he is of course terrific muttering the deadpan quips supplied by Tom Mankiewicz. The film has an enjoyably surreal atmosphere at times with the desert sequences and the famous Moon Buggysetpiece (Bond encountering a 'moon landing' in a television studio seems to be an early reference to those conspiracy theories that the moon landing was hoaxed). The score by John Barry is appropriately strange and makes a nice sonic backdrop for the action.

One of the disappointing things about Diamonds Are Forever though is that it barely mentions the events of OHMSS (where Blofeld and his goons murdered Bond's wife). Despite the return of Connery, part of you wishes Diamonds Are Forever was a direct follow-up to OHMSS with Lazenby. Diamonds Are Forever, with its humour and camp (Blofeld resorts to drag at one point), set the tone for the seventies Bond films to come. You could argue that Diamonds Are Forever sometimes feels a lot like the first Roger Moore Bond film - only without Roger Moore.

CHAPTER TWO - BECOMING BOND

Before production began on the next Bond film - Live and Let Die - Tom Mankiewicz had lunch with Sean Connery in a charm offensive that EON hoped might persuade Connery to do the film. It was of course unsuccessful. "I always hear that it's my ******* obligation to play James Bond," Connery told Mankiewicz. "I've done six, when does my ******* obligation stop? After ten, twelve, fifteen?" Despite the best efforts of United Artists, Sean Connery decided that Diamonds Are Forever was definitely the end of his association with James Bond - until 1983 at least. He had grown weary of the role in the 1960s and found the fame and attention increasingly constrictive. As Connery pointed out, The Beatles had their fame spread over four people whereas with the James Bond craze it was him all on his own.

Connery simply wanted to do other things as an actor now. He didn't want to keep endlessly playing the same character all the time. It is said that United Artists (obviously to no avail) offered Connery $5 million to star in Live and Let Die. After they finished Diamonds Are Forever, the producers had the idea of bringing back Ursula Andress as Honey Ryder in the next movie. However, when Sean Connery made it clear he would not be coming back this idea was shelved. There wasn't much point in bringing back Ursula Andress if Connery wasn't doing the movie because it wouldn't be a Bond reunion anymore.

The familiar Bond casting circus now kicked into gear yet again. United Artists wanted a Hollywood star like Robert Redford or Clint Eastwood - but these were unrealistic suggestions. Redford was one of the biggest stars in Hollywood at the time so why would he want to constrict himself to Bond films when he had his pick of projects anyway? Clint Eastwood said he was offered big money to do Bond but he had no interest in the part at all. It just wasn't his cup of tea.

The late Michael Winner (best known for directing the first three Death Wish movies with Charles Bronson) claimed in his memoir that he turned down the chance to direct Live and Let Die. Winner said he later regretted this decision. "I don't know why I turned down James Bond. I can't imagine. I took the call right there, 1971. 'Are you interested in James Bond?' they said. 'Harry Saltzman would like you to do it.' I said, 'No.' I mean, it's not as if I was making Hamlet! Oh, no thanks, I only do Ibsen! I was only doing thrillers anyway. A moment of lunacy."

The director Guy Hamilton assumed that he was done with the Bond franchise after Diamonds Are Forever but he was persuaded to come back for Live and Let Die and once again found himself in charge of a film that had no leading man. Hamilton decided to have a bash at finding a Bond actor himself and remembered someone who he thought would be perfect. During the production of Diamonds Are Forever in the United States, Hamilton and the Bond producers had been introduced to the actor Burt Reynolds. Reynolds was in his mid-thirties and about to make the John Boorman film Deliverance at the time.

Guy Hamilton thought that Reynolds was terrific. The actor was good looking, tough, and could be charming and funny. In 1972, Hamilton proposed that they simply cast Burt Reynolds as Bond in Live and Let Die. The interest in Burt Reynolds was such that his agent was permitted to read the script for Live and Let Die. In the end though it was a combination of Cubby Broccoli and cold feet from Reynolds that stopped him from becoming the third official James Bond actor. Tom Mankiewicz said that Saltzman and Hamilton were happy to cast Reynolds but Cubby had second thoughts and insisted that Bond should be played by a British actor - which was something of a contradiction because Cubby had only recently cast an Australian and American as Bond! As for Burt Reynolds, he was always reticent about taking the role and eventually backed out.

John Richardson, who was nearly cast as Bond in OHMSS, was brought back and considered afresh for Live and Let Die. Richardson was about thirty-eight years old and was about to begin his era of making low-budget Italian films. He had though been in the 1970 Barbara Streisand film On a Clear Day You Can See Forever. Richardson was still a very handsome man and with the right toupee would have been a terrific looking Bond. However, it was not to be for Richardson and he did not get the part again.

The other familiar names back in the fray for Live and Let Die naturally included the inimitable David Warbeck. Warbeck's test was to no avail and once again he failed to find the winning numbers for the 007 casting sweepstakes. Warbeck later claimed that he was told he would become Bond if Roger Moore couldn't get free of his Persuaders contract but one must probably take this with a pinch of salt. All the evidence suggests that Michael Billington was Roger's closest rival - not David Warbeck.

Also back to test again was Patrick Mower. Mower said that he tested again for Bond in the early seventies but lost out to Roger Moore. This would obviously indicate that Mower was a candidate for Live and Let Die. At the time, Mower had recently appeared in the film Incense for the Damned (with Peter Cushing) and also Jason King and Black Beauty on television. Patrick Mower was one of those actors who never stopped working but had yet to find the role which propelled him to the next level. James Bond would obviously have done that but the 007 role would remain frustratingly elusive for Mower. The young Patrick Mower probably would have made a decent fist of Bond. There were certainly worse candidates down the decades.

John Ronane was another actor who was considered for Live and Let Die. Ronane was about thirty-eight at the time and had appeared in films such as King Rat and Charlie Bubbles. His many television credits included (of course) The Avengers and The Saint. It seems slightly odd that if the producers liked

Ronane they hadn't considered him for Diamonds Are Forever or OHMSS. Maybe they did. Ronane was not what you would describe as traditionally handsome or screamingly James Bondian in terms of looks but there was obviously something about him that EON liked. Ronane apparently did well in the Live and Let Die casting sweepstakes and was a serious candidate. He later moved to the United States and taught acting before returning home and appearing in TV shows like Juliet Bravo and Howard's Way.

Very near the top of the EON wish list for Live and Let Die was Jon Finch. Finch was a brooding 30 year-old actor who resembled the wayward love child of Oliver Reed and Timothy Dalton (Finch and Dalton sometimes even found themselves up for the same parts because of their similarities). Horror films The Vampire Lovers and The Horror of Frankenstein put Finch on the map and then he appeared in Roman Polanski's Macbeth and Alfred Hitchcock's brilliant suspense thriller Frenzy.

Finch was quite an intense actor (note how Finch refuses to make his innocent wronged character in Frenzy sympathetic at all!) with a rich theatrical anachronistic voice. Not only that but he was a former paratrooper so the 007 style fights and stunts were not likely to be a problem at all. Finch even raced cars in his spare time. He was a pretty good candidate but - alas - he simply wasn't interested. A few years later Finch turned down a lead role in Richard Lester's The Three Musketeers. Jon Finch was clearly not that bothered about money and fame - which probably explains why he never became a big star.

It seems that John Gavin was looked at again for Live and Let Die although he doesn't appear to have been a serious candidate this time. It could be that Cubby Broccoli brought Gavin back into the 007 casting loop as a courtesy more than anything. If United Artists didn't like Gavin's casting in 1970 they were unlikely to have changed their minds two years later. It is sometimes alleged that George Lazenby was a contender for Live and Let Die - which would have been pretty strange! Although Lazenby was only in his early thirties his career was on life support and he said he suffered from alcoholism and two nervous breakdowns around this time. It seems very unlikely that United Artists and Cubby Broccoli would have welcomed Lazenby's return as Bond. As far as they were concerned Lazenby had burned his bridges.

Jeremy Brett (who became most famous for playing Sherlock Holmes on television in the 1980s) was another actor in contention for Live and Let Die. Brett may well have been considered for OHMSS too. Brett was nearly forty years-old in 1972 and an accomplished stage actor. He was probably best known at this time for appearing in the film My Fair Lady. Harry Saltzman was said to have been a big fan of Brett after watching My Fair lady and was an advocate of him doing Bond. Brett was tall, dark-haired and handsome and looked rather like the John McLusky sketch of Bond commissioned by Ian Fleming. It appears though that Cubby Broccoli wasn't so sold on Brett. It is possible that Broccoli thought that Brett might be a little too mannered and fey for Bond. There is no doubt that Brett would have been capable of the elegance and cruelty of Bond but would he have been tough enough?

Anthony Hopkins has said that he was approached by Cubby Broccoli with a view to playing James Bond in Live and Let Die. Hopkins was about 34 at the time and had just made the spy film When Eight Bells Toll. In the film Hopkins played British Treasury secret agent Phillip Calvert. The idea was that this would be the first in a new franchise of Phillip Calvert films but this never transpired in the end. The ironic thing is that when Eight Bells Toll was designed to be a new gritty spy franchise to fill the gap left by Bond - which rival studios wrongly considered to be on its last legs and doomed without Sean Connery! Hopkins said that while it was very flattering to be approached about James Bond he did not pursue the part because he didn't feel he was right for it.

In the end only two actors were left standing after all the

interviews, auditions, and 007 screen tests for Live and Let Die. One of these was Michael Billington. As far as James Bond goes, it could be said that the unlucky Billington was truly always a bridesmaid and never the bride. Billington was 31 at the time and appearing in the TV show The Onedin Line. He had previously appeared in the Gerry Anderson sci-fi television show UFO. Billington played Colonel Paul Foster in UFO. He was sort of like a Lewis Collins style action man in the show. Billington didn't especially like UFO though and was fearful of being typecast in this sort of part. He took a part in The Onedin line because he got to play a dubious rogue - and thus move away from his UFO image. Billington was ambitious and took the craft of acting seriously but his hairy chested Milk Tray man looks tended to make people think he could only be an action hero.

Though he had been looked at before by Harry Saltzman near the end of the OHMSS casting, Live and Let Die was the first time that Michael Billington actually did a screen test for James Bond. "I heard that Cubby Broccoli wanted to meet me with the prospect of a screen test," said Billington. "I was somewhat surprised. I was having some success on British Television at the time but really wanted to do a quality movie. I think I did well on the test for Live And Let Die and liked Guy Hamilton, the director. The scene was a specially written scene, which I played with an actress called Caroline Seymour." Gratuitous trivia - Caroline Seymour played Harold's stripper wife Zita in the first Steptoe & Son film. She later appeared in all manner of things - including Star Trek: The Next Generation and Space 1999.

At one point during the Live and Let Die casting process, Michael Billington believed he actually had the part. His agent told him that an offer and contracts were being prepared and there was also speculation in the newspapers that Billington would soon be announced as the new Bond. Billington was to be disappointed though - and at the final hurdle too. At time fell short, the decision was made to cast Roger Moore as the new James Bond in Live and Let Die. "When it was announced that Roger Moore was going to do it, I was stunned," said Billington. Billington had a feeling though that this wouldn't be his last brush with James Bond and he certainly turned out to be right about that.

Roger Moore had played a shrewd game when it came to James Bond. During the production of his TV show The Persuaders a few years before, Roger had mingled with the Bond cast and crew because they were shooting parts of Diamonds Are Forever at the same studio. Roger had learned on pretty good authority that Connery definitely wasn't coming back and that the part of Bond would be up for grabs again in the next film. When he heard this, Moore declined Lew Grade's offer to sign up for another series of The Persuaders so that he would be available for James Bond - should it be offered to him.

Roger's children used to go swimming with Harry Saltzman's children and he knew Cubby Broccoli from gentlemen's clubs in London. You could sort of say Roger had the inside track on Bond. He already knew the producers quite well and they were aware that Roger Moore could be a safe pair of hands at a time when the franchise faced an uncertain future and couldn't really afford to take too many risks. Roger was 45 by the time Live and Let Die went into production. This was definitely his last chance of playing Bond because he would be too old the next time it came around. Roger was delighted to have bagged the part. He wasn't a reluctant Bond in the slightest.

Roger said that Broccoli and Saltzman ordered him to cut his hair and lose weight in preparation for Bond. This advice obviously worked because Roger looks terrific in Live and Let Die. There seems to be some evidence though that Cubby Broccoli and Harry Saltzman were not entirely 100% convinced by Roger Moore and might have preferred Michael Billington to be cast as Bond in Live and Let Die. The story goes that United Artists disagreed. They did not want another unknown (Billington was not completely unknown but he was hardly world famous) actor and so voted for Roger Moore over

Billington.

The director Guy Hamilton was, according to legend, given the deciding vote and he too preferred Roger Moore over Michael Billington. In the end the casting of Roger Moore made a lot of sense. He was a very experienced actor and fairly famous already because of his stint playing Simon Templar on television. On the plus side, Roger Moore was 6'2, still handsome and well known to international audiences. He was adept at heroic roles with a penchant for light humour. He could conceivably be a shrewd compromise choice and carry Bond into and through the seventies.

On the minus side, Roger was 45 and would be seen by Bond purists as lightweight and a departure from the Connery/Lazenby model. You could probably say that pragmatism triumphed in this case. Roger was not a bold or offbeat choice for Bond. He was primarily seen as someone who would be less risky than another relative unknown. Roger Moore signed a three film 007 contract and later admitted that he suspected the Bond franchise was nearing its end anyway and that he might not even get to do a third film.

It has been alleged that Michael Billington was also 'retained' on an unofficial sort of contract in case they needed a new Bond again sooner than expected. Billington would remain close to the Broccoli family and even have a relationship with Cubby's daughter Barbara Broccoli. Whenever there was any doubt about Roger's participation in the next Bond movie, it was Michael Billington who Cubby would call and have waiting in the wings. It is doubtful that there is anyone who came as close to playing Bond so many times as Michael Billington.

Roger was the oldest actor to win the role of James Bond but - strangely enough - in Live and Let Die he could pass for the youngest. He looks incredibly boyish and youthful in the film at times. His Bond tenure was rather like The Saint on a much bigger budget. Moore's time as Bond wasn't exactly radical but it was fun. Roger Moore went on to make seven films (a record that is unlikely to ever be broken) and miraculously proved that the Bond franchise was a perfectly viable ongoing commodity even without Sean Connery.

When he was told that he had been chosen to become James Bond, Roger Moore said he celebrated by having oysters and martinis with the director Guy Hamilton. Roger said he had no reservations whatsoever about taking over as James Bond. He said it was like playing Hamlet in that there were others before him and would be others after him. As was custom in the Bond series (OHMSS notwithstanding), the next movie would share a title and character names with an Ian Fleming novel but little besides that.

Live and Let Die was the second James Bond novel written by Ian Fleming and originally published in 1954. The plot of the book begins with gold coins from seventeenth century pirate Henry Morgan turning up in the United States and being sold to fund the Soviet spy network there. The operation is masterminded by SMERSH operative 'Mr Big', mysterious and feared boss of the black underworld. James Bond is dispatched to New York by M to investigate where he teams up with old friend Felix Leiter - now working as an FBI/CIA liaison officer - and is soon up to his neck in intrigue and danger in locations as diverse as Harlem, St Petersburg and Jamaica.

It's fair to say that Fleming's second Bond book is more quickly paced and larger in scope than the first Bond novel Casino Royale. We get the first sense of Bond as an international globetrotter and his investigation of Mr Big is interesting because we learn that Big rules by fear with a network of voices reporting anything to him. He's quite a sinister character and we often feel an element of danger for Bond as he seeks to get more information. Big uses voodoo superstitions to control the black population and keeps fortune teller Solitare close by and although the voodoo elements are a bit hokey it does inject an air of the exotic into the book. In typical Fleming fashion we also get a lot of information presented to us about voodoo ('The next step [he read] is the invocation of evil denizens of the Voodoo pantheon...') and indeed the history of Henry Morgan.

As you'd expect from a Fleming though the story is exciting and there are plenty of entertaining and tense moments like a duel with a robber in a warehouse and an atmospheric night swim to a Caribbean island by Bond where he is literally swimming with the sharks. The author's tendency to 'recap' is a tad unnecessary at times but he creates a vivid fifties atmosphere and the scenes in Harlem are always interesting. Live and Let Die though is somewhat dated and patronising at times in its depiction of black people and some moments are a tad jarring for the modern reader - especially Fleming's attempts at black 'slang'.

It's interesting to read the sections in the book which were later used for the film series. An attack on Leiter in Live and Let Die was used in the film Licence To Kill and another famous set-piece where Bond and Solitaire are tied up and face the prospect of being keelhauled over coral underwater was borrowed for For You Eyes Only. One thing I quite like about the books - which they understandably tend to avoid in the films - is that they reference real people from the era in which they were written. An example here being the legendary boxer Sugar Ray Robinson who gets a mention during the Harlem sections. 'Let's hope we both know when to stop when the time comes,' says Leiter to Bond - in reference to Sugar Ray boxing well into the veteran phase.

Solitaire is a typically alluring Bond girl although perhaps not as interesting or complex as Vesper Lynd in Casino Royale. 'Her face was pale, with the pallor of white families that have lived long in the tropics,' writes Fleming. 'But it contained no trace of the usual exhaustion which the tropics impart to the skin and hair. The eyes were blue, alight and disdainful, but, as they gazed into his with a touch of humour, he realized they contained some message for him personally.' The perpetually laughing Tee-Hee is a decent henchman and the use of Felix Leiter here is nicely done. The friendship between Leiter and

Bond really comes through in this book and we see that the two men have much in common. Bond's reaction to Leiter's trouble is quite poignant in Live and Let Die. Despite dated elements, Live and Let Die is an entertaining and interesting book with some good set-pieces that builds to a suspenseful finale.

CHAPTER THREE - LIVE AND LET DIE

The writer Tom Manciwiecz lobbied for Diana Ross to play Solitare in Live and Let Die. It is alleged that United Artists though were not comfortable at the thought of a black female lead in a Bond film (this was 1972 when times were, sadly, very different). Catherine Deneuve was considered for the part of Solitare - as were Helen Mirren and Goldie Hawn. Mirren and Hawn were not interested in doing a James Bond film though and passed. Gayle Hunnicutt was eventually the original choice to play Solitaire in Live and Let Die but had to pull out when she became pregnant.

In the end, 20 year-old English actress Jane Seymour was cast as Solitare after Cubby Broccoli saw her in The Onedin Line (a show he was probably watching to cast an eye over Michael Billington). Tom Mankiewicz (who wrote the script) felt that Jane Seymour was miscast as Solitare in Live and Let Die. Mankiewicz felt that Seymour looked far too young and innocent and this made it seem as if Bond was taking advantage of her. Jane Seymour turned down the role of Solitare twice before relenting and taking the part. Seymour said she had no particular ambition to be in a Bond film but took the part in the end because she had run out of money and couldn't afford to buy a new coat!

Yaphet Kotto was cast as the villain in Live and Let Die. Guy Hamilton later said he didn't like Yaphet Kotto very much when he directed the film. "Yaphet Kotto, I regret bitterly. I did not enjoy working with him at all. Originally it was to be a very distinguished American black actor. Suddenly Harry Saltzman announced he's out and UA say Yaphet Kotto is really hot property. We were forced into Yaphet Kotto. I'd never met him until he turned up on the set. He starts off thinking he should be playing Bond - quite seriously. He was very badly behaved, he would try and make life difficult."

The dislike went both ways as Yaphet Kotto had few good things to say about Live and Let Die in later years. Kotto complained that he was shut out of the publicity and hype for the movie. "They didn't play my character up. That hurt me a lot, man. I went through a lot of goddamn emotional hell because they were afraid people would be angry that a black guy was not being Sidney Poitier. I was the opposite of everything he created." The black actress Gloria Hendry (who plays Rosie) was removed from the promotional art for Live and Let Die in apartheid South Africa. Roger Moore even received racist hate mail because of his kissing scenes with Gloria Hendry in Live and Let Die. Hendry said that Roger Moore was a charming co-star and even shared his limo with her on location in the West Indies.

Geoffrey Holder, who plays Baron Samedi in Live and Let Die, had a fear of snakes. Making this snake festooned movie was no picnic for him. Geoffrey Holder also choreographed the voodoo scenes in Live and Let Die. The end of Live and Let Die, with the (seemingly ghostly) Baron Samedi on the front of the train, was included with a view to bringing the character back but this obviously never happened in the end. Live and Let Die is one of the few 007 films where Bond and Felix Leiter have a believable easygoing chemistry. This is because Roger Moore and David Hedison were friends in real life. Hedison would, somewhat incongruously, return as Leiter many years later alongside Timothy Dalton in Licence To Kill.

Madeline Smith was only paid £100 to play Miss Caruso in Live and Let Die. Miss Caruso is the missing Italian agent who has her dress unzipped by Bond's magnetic watch. "It was a tiny amount," said Smith. "You hardly got anything at all in those days. But I was 23, and it was a wonderful experience. I absolutely loved Roger Moore. I could not believe it when I got the part. I never even auditioned for it. I had been in an episode of The Persuaders, which Roger had directed, and unbeknown to me, he suggested me for the part." Madeline Smith said she felt somewhat uncomfortable shooting the scenes in Live and Let Die when her character Miss Caruso is cosying up to Bond because Roger Moore's wife was on the set that day watching them do the scene! As far as Bond Girls go, in 1972 the media had reported that Playboy model Linda Summers was set for a big role in Live and Let Die but this turned out to be idle tittle tattle with no basis in fact.

Series regulars Bernard Lee and Lois Maxwell were back as M and Moneypenny respectively but - strangely - there is no appearance in Live and Let Die for Desmond Llewelyn as Q. Llewelyn had arranged some time off from the television show Follyfoot to make Live and Let Die so he was rather irritated to learn that Broccoli and Saltzman didn't want Q to appear in the film. Why didn't they want Q? The general theory is that they wanted to eschew gadgets in this film but that doesn't make sense because Live and Let Die has plenty of gadgets. It is more the case that EON simply desired, for this picture at least, not to saddle Roger with the trappings of the Connery years. Tuxedo, casinos, Dom Pérignon, Aston Martin, and Q!

Bernard Lee was still grieving from the death of his wife at the time of Live and Let Die so Kenneth Moore was lined up as a replacement M. Lee did the film in the end though.

Clifton James was cast as the bumbling and cartoonish Sheriff J.W. Pepper in the movie. It was Tom Manciwiecz who came up with this comic relief character. Manciwiecz said that Guy Hamilton thought the Sheriff J.W. Pepper was really funny so kept expanding the screen time of Clifton James in the movie. So, if you are one of those Bond fans who doesn't like Sheriff J.W. Pepper then you know who to blame!

Guy Hamilton told Roger to forget all about Sean Connery and just play the part his own way. Roger's Bond was unavoidably going to be lighter in tone than Connery but his humour and style was expected to make up for that. Roger Moore might not have been the most forceful actor ever but he was more believable than Sean or George as a fashion expert and someone who would know his way around an outrageously expensive wine list. Fleming's literary James Bond dislikes killing (despite it obviously being an unavoidable part of his job) and Roger said he always kept this in mind in his portrayal. As a consequence, Moore's Bond was less brutal than the others.

'It was part of his profession to kill people,' wrote Fleming. 'He had never liked doing it and when he had to kill he did it as well as he knew how and forgot about it. As a secret agent who held the rare double-O prefix - the licence to kill in the Secret Service - it was his duty to be as cool about death as a surgeon. If it happened, it happened. Regret was unprofessional - worse, it was death-watch beetle in the soul.'

While he was shooting Live and Let Die, Roger agreed to keep a diary detailing his experiences for a book. The book came out in 1973 and was titled Roger Moore's James Bond Diary. Roger apparently dictated his diary into a tape recorder at the end of each day and then it was typed up and edited for the book. 'It began on Sunday, 8 October 1972,' begins Moore. 'When, as the new James Bond, I left England in a blaze of publicity for the first location in New Orleans. We flew via New York and the journey was hysterical. Danny Kaye was aboard and he started on the stewardesses straight away. While the girl was standing up in front of the jumbo jet trying to show everybody how to put on a life jacket, there was Danny sitting there miming exactly what the poor girl was doing.'

The book is a great insight into the huge logistical operation involved in putting together a James Bond film with tons of equipment flying to different corners of the world with the various crews and always of particular interest to Bond fans who have probably seen the finished film countless times. It is of course also always pleasant and enjoyable to be in the warm and witty company of the self-deprecating Roger Moore as he dispenses anecdotes, sends himself up, plays practical jokes on Yaphet Kotto, and also details his social life during the shoot with various famous people - some in the film and some not - flitting in and out of the diary. Not many people, I suspect, can say, as Moore does here, that Kirk Douglas turned up at his house in Denham on Christmas Day to say hello!

Moore's first days of filming as the new 007 concern the famous speedboat chase sequence in a Louisiana bayou and the actor manages to have an accident fairly swiftly into the shoot that leaves him with a dodgy leg and a fractured tooth. 'How on earth did I get myself into this situation?' muses Moore, who then jokes that he might end up playing Bond with no teeth at this rate! Moore's passages about being signed to become the new Bond and his thoughts on the prospect are always very interesting with some fascinating titbits for 007 fans who have followed the series for as long as they can remember.

'When I first knew was going to do Bond,' says Moore. 'Harry Saltzman, who co-produces with Cubby Broccoli, said it must be kept secret but he wanted me to meet the director Guy Hamilton. We met at Scott's in Mayfair, in true Bond-style. I confessed to Guy that in reading the script I could only ever hear Sean's voice saying; "My name is Bond." In fact, as I vocalized to myself I found I was giving it a Scottish accent!' Hamilton tells Moore that Sean was Sean and he will do it in his own way and that's about all there is to it.

The process of making a film is always quite surprising when the mechanics are laid bare. Moore, for example, is on set for weeks before he even gets a couple of lines of dialogue to say and one of the very last things he shoots is the scene with the lovely Madeline Smith where Bond uses his magnetic LED watch to unzip her dress in his flat - a scene that actually begins the finished film after the title sequence. This takes place in a slightly chilly and draughty Pinewood set and Moore's account of shooting the scene is very funny at times. 'It may seem like money for jam pressed close to the beautiful Madeline Smith and taking her clothes off into the bargain, but on the twentieth take your arm is aching, you've got cramp in your left foot and you're right knee is going to sleep. When I got home the children asked me what I did today and I wasn't quite sure what to tell them. I could hardly say I was in bed

with a lady this morning and I made twenty attempts to take
her dress off!'

There are some great anecdotes in the diaries. When Moore's
good friend David Hedison arrives to play Felix Leiter, Moore
confesses that he always greets Hedison by mimicking his
famous last line in the original version The Fly. I loved the
story too where Moore's young son asks him if he could beat
up James Bond and Moore patiently explains that he is James
Bond now. 'I know that,' sighs his son. 'I mean the real James
Bond...Sean Connery.' Moore is always generous and warm
towards his co-stars and there are some interesting titbits
scattered through the book.

Jane Seymour arrives in between her commitments on the
television series The Onedin Line - where Cubby and Harry
first spotted her - and Yaphet Kotto, who plays the villain Mr
Big, gives a 'black power salute' during his first 007 photo call.
'Whether he was serious or not I don't know,' says Moore. 'But
the sequel was a scorching row.' Moore is soon fond of Kotto
though and playing jokes on him. He's also gushing in his
praise for Geoffrey Holder and Gloria Hendry. 'A little light
has gone out of our lives with the leaving of lovely Gloria who
has completed her scenes and gone off on an Austrian holiday
where her warm exuberance is probably melting the mountain
snow.' Roger reprints a mad racist letter in the diaries he
received from some bigoted woman telling him she always
followed his career since The Saint but will no longer do so
because he's canoodling onscreen with a black actress.

Interestingly, Harry Saltzman features in the diary far more
than fellow Bond producer Cubby Broccoli. The pair seemed to
sort of alternate on the Bond films it appears and Live and Let
Die was largely overseen by Saltzman - who comes across as a
colourful character who, not unlike 007, is rather fastidious
about his food and drink and the social aspects of shooting.
'Outside it was about ninety degrees as I washed my Creole
shrimps down with a very nice light American beer,' says
Moore. 'Harry, and Jackie his wife, were helping theirs down

with a white wine but Harry was screaming because it wasn't the Chablis he had ordered to be put on ice.' Moore says that Cubby Broccoli once said that if the gourmet Harry Saltzman had been at the Last Supper he probably would have sent it back!

Roger tells an amusing story about Broccoli too when Cubby arrives on the set. Broccoli brought a journalist from London who he had invited to dinner. The journalist was unaware that Cubby's invitation to dinner was at a plush New Orlean's restaurant 4,000 miles away! The meal was probably worth it suggests Moore. One other enjoyable aspect to the book are the descriptions of the various locales, especially when the production moves to the West Indies and Moore is living in a plush residence and taking a swim each morning before filming. 'From the terrace of our two bedroomed split-level apartment set in the hillside I can hear the limpid caribbean waters below lapping the pink terracotta walls. Terraced walks surround two azure swimming pools and tropical flowers of every hue peek out of the palm fronds and lush green vegetation. Multi-coloured birds, competing with the flowers for beauty, chirp cheerfully; and why not? They know they are living in Paradise.'

Roger Moore not only fractured a tooth but also suffered from kidney stones when production began on Live and Let Die. He certainly wouldn't be the last Bond actor to suffer for his art! The movie was no picnic for Jane Seymour either as she suffered a bout of dysentery shooting Live and Let Die in Jamaica. Roger had to go to a bus depot in London to learn how to drive a double-decker bus before he made Live and Let Die. Seventeen boats were destroyed in the stunt rehearsals for the film. It was very chilly at Pinewood Studios when they shot some of the bedroom scenes for Bond and Solitare in Live and Let Die so Roger Moore and Jane Seymour wore football socks in bed to stay warm.

It took twenty-nine takes to shoot the moment in Live and Let Die when Bond unzips Miss Caruso's dress with his magnetic watch. Roger named this watch as his favourite Bond gadget. Kanaga in the film is named after the real-life owner of the crocodile farm. The crew got the idea of using the crocodile farm in the movie when they stumbled across a sign that read - Trespassers Will Be Eaten. The famous crocodile stunt in Live and Let Die was a late replacement for a planned sequence where Bond nearly meets his end in a giant coffee bean milling machine. This would appear to explain why they go to great lengths early on in the film to show that Bond has an espresso coffee machine in his flat. It was meant to anticipate the punchline of a later sequence.

During the production of Live and Let Die, the Bond team had to pay 'protection' money to shoot in a rough part of Harlem. Roger Moore said he had a Tarot card reading when he made Live and Let Die. The cards predicted he would perish in an accident involving a black car. Roger said he avoided black cars for quite a long time after that reading! John Barry could not compose the music in Live and Let Die because he was working on a musical based on Billy Liar. Paul McCartney wrote the theme song and performed it with his band Wings. George Martin, the 'fifth Beatle', was hired to compose the music and did a fine job too.

So what of Live and Let Die the film? How does it stack up these days? The new 007 is absent from the unusual pre-credit sequence which (after a funky 1970's gunbarrel) features a series of murders from the United Nations HQ in New York to a small Caribbean island called San Monique. All of the victims are agents attempting to find out more about the mysterious Dr Kananga, the dictator of San Monique (played with relish by the imposing Yaphet Kotto). Cue one of Maurice Binder's best title sequences and Paul McCartney's memorable theme song. Both are a departure in style from what had come before and they work very well.

In another departure, our first glimpse of Bond finds him in his London flat. Woken by someone at the door he checks the time on his Pulsar P2 digital watch and we see that he is in bed

with 1970's horror/comedy icon Madeline Smith, here playing
Italian agent Miss Caruso. Bond finds M when he opens the
door and after a classic raised eye-brow moment from Roger,
007 uses his espresso machine to make his bemused boss
some coffee.

007 also has a Magnetic watch (Rolex Submariner) brought to
him by Miss Moneypenny from Q Branch. When switched on
Bond's watch generates a powerful magnetic field strong
enough to deflect a bullet. He demonstrates this by making
M's teaspoon fly away from his cup. Miss Moneypenny bails
007 out by helping to divert M away from the wardrobe Miss
Caruso is hiding in and Bond uses his watch's magnetic
abilities to unzip Madeline Smith's dress. The new Bond is
considerably lighter in tone and less physical than his
predecessors but more urbane with a great sense of humour.

Bond is sent to New York where the first agent was killed and
where Dr Kananga is at the UN. The very 1970's music score is
great fun and we hear the voice of Solitaire (Jane Seymour) as
Bond's plane takes off and he arrives in New York. As soon as
Bond arrives his driver is killed while taking him to meet Felix
Leiter (David Hedison) in an entertaining sequence during
which 007 attempts to take control of the car from the back-
seat. The trail leads Bond to Mr Big, a gangster who runs a
chain of Fillet of Soul restaurants. Bond meets Solitaire, a
tarot expert who has the ability to see both the future and
remote events in the present.

Bond follows Kananga back to San Monique with CIA agent
Rosie Carver where he seduces Solitaire. Their love had been
foretold in the cards, but was rigged up by Bond, having
created a deck entirely of "The Lovers" cards, which by
"compelling to earthly love" takes away her power. Bond is
helped by Quarrel Jr (Roy Stewart), and for those who
remember, Bond had a friend in Jamaica named Quarrel from
Dr No. Rosie turns out to be a double-agent on Kananga's
payroll and Bond and Solitare escape with the aid of a London
double-decker bus but not before stumbling across poppy

fields. It transpires that Kananga is producing large quantities of heroin and is protecting the poppy fields by using the locals belief and fear of voodoo and the occult.

Bond heads to New Orleans and is captured by Mr Big - who is revealed to be Kananga in a very unconvincing mask. Kananga is distributing heroin under the guise of Mr Big. 007 escapes and is chased across the Louisina bayous in the famous speedboat sequence. He then heads back to rescue Solitare from San Monique and survives capture in Kananga's underground complex and a train fight with Kananga's henchman Tee Hee (he of the metal claw for a hand). "Just being disarming darling." In the closing scene of the film, the central voodoo character, Baron Samedi, is seen perched on the front of the speeding train laughing.

Live and Let Die was essentially the first reboot for the Bond series. It was sensibly decided not to saddle Roger Moore with too many of the staples associated with Sean Connery and subsequently the film feels like a slightly strange entry. There is no Q and Bond does not order a martini or swan about in a tuxedo. There is no Aston Martin and Bond, like Roger Moore, smokes cigars. The film seems less lavish than some other entries and the world threatening supervillain is replaced by a more down to Earth baddie with far more modest and 'real' world aims. Live and Let Die was released during the height of the 1970s Blaxploitation era and uses actors from this period with mixed results. Live and Let Die lurches around in tone somewhat though never quite to the point where the viewer risks tonal whiplash.

Gloria Hendry is required to shriek a bit too much for my liking and some of the street jive black stereotypes seem very dated and dubious now but Julius Harris is suitably menacing as Tee Hee and Geoffrey Holder throws himself into his Baron Samedi role. Like Jaws, Clifton James as Sheriff J.W. Pepper ("What are boy? Some kind of doomsday machine!") is a character that you could only imagine appearing in the Roger Moore era. There are three major chase sequences in Live and

Let Die and they are all great fun although the boat and double-decker bus chase could have been more tightly edited. The airport scene is an amusing and typical Roger Moore era escapade and ends with a funny line delivered deadpan by 007.

The action when it arrives does seem a bit stretched out and there are parts of the film that seem slightly incoherent and stilted but overall Live and Let Die is a hugely entertaining film. George Martin is one of the best of the non-Barry composers and he works the theme song into the film to good effect. Jane Seymour does well as the innocent Solitare and from first scene to last, Roger Moore is never less than polished, likable and often very funny. His fight with Tee Hee at the end of the film never fails to make me smile. Worst bit? Kananga's death as any Bond fan will tell you! Best bit? Bond's escape from the crocodiles - which is cool, unflappable and ingenious in the best tradition of the cinematic character. Bond's ingenuity in evading the crocs while stranded in the pond is a great moment because we expect his magnetic watch to get him out of trouble but he has to rely on his wits instead.

It's fascinating to see the series waveringly grope its way into a new decade and I like Roger in Live and Let Die. He comes across as a jet-setting playboy who has been recruited into the secret service. Roger looks much younger and trimmer in the movie than Sean did in Diamonds Are Forever. Live and Let Die has some slightly jarring shifts in tone and is very much a lucky dip but the boat chase sequences are exciting and the horror elements not without charm. Live and Let Die is atypical and strange enough to be considered mildly cultish today and is generally a solid reboot for the franchise. It draws a line under Sean Connery era more successfully than was anticipated and has enough wit and action to satisfy most viewers and fans. The film is not perfect but it is an interesting and perfectly acceptable first go around for Roger as the world's most famous spy.

CHAPTER FOUR - THE MAN WITH THE GOLDEN GUN

Live and Let Die was released in the United States at the end of June 1973 and had its world premiere at the Odeon Leicester Square on the 6th of July. HRH Princess Anne attended the premiere as the Royal guest and celebrities attending the premiere included Michael Caine, Peter Sellers, Gregory Peck, David Frost, David Bowie, and Lulu. Burt Reynolds was also among the celebrities there that night. Had things turned out differently, Reynolds could easily have been playing Bond in the film they were about to watch!

The trailer promised audiences "More excitement, more action. Much more... Roger Moore!" The promotional art with George Lazenby had billed James Bond as the star of OHMSS but it was all different now. Live and Let Die's posters were confident enough to boldly declare Roger Moore AS James Bond. This is why they had gone for a 'name' actor rather than another unknown. It's a bit unfair to compare Michael Billington to Lazenby because Billington was a fairly experienced (in comparison to George) and competent actor but Roger Moore was simply much better known than Billington and this is why he was picked. It was a reaction to the producers having their fingers burned with the strange Lazenby affair.

The value of having a well known and highly professional actor as Bond was evident during the promotional tour for Live and Let Die. Roger Moore hit the chat show circuit and charmed audiences in his usual droll and self-deprecating fashion. Roger said that he wasn't Sean Connery and so didn't try to impersonate him as Bond. "Next to Sean," said Roger, "I'm a comedian. Sean is a great actor, that's all there is to it. I can never do what he has done outside of Bond. Simon Templar - The Saint - was a boy scout compared to Bond. But I really enjoyed doing Live and Let Die. It was a rough film - but fun."

Apparently, Roger's Bond contract stipulated that he wasn't allowed to play a spy or secret agent in any other (non Bond) movies. Roger quipped to a newspaper that he might have to start playing villains to get work! The promotional campaign for Live and Let Die was excellent. There was a commercial deal with a razor brand, viewmaster slides, toys, commercial tie-ins with luxury boat and car brands, and more besides. Jane Seymour and Gloria Henry also had profiles in Playboy magazine to drum up interest in the movie.

The reviews of Live and Let Die were something of a mixed bag to say the least. You could argue that Live and Let Die is actually more appreciated now than when it came out. Live and Let Die, perhaps as a consequence of its strange tone and horror elements, is actually quite cultish today and figures like Sam Mendes and Daniel Craig have said it was their first Bond and one they always loved. When Live and Let Die was released in 1973, Richard Schickel in Time Magazine though felt the movie was somewhat troubling in its attitudes to race. "Why are all the blacks either stupid brutes or primitives deep into the occult and voodooism? Why is miscegenation so often used as a turn-on? Why do such questions even arise in what is supposed to be pure entertainment?"

Roger Ebert also gave Live and Let Die a lukewarm review when it came out in 1973. 'Live and Let Die is the ninth James Bond picture, and not exactly the best. It has all the necessary girls, gimmicks, subterranean control rooms, uniformed goons and magic wristwatches it can hold, but it doesn't have the wit and it doesn't have the style of the best Bond movies. This may have something to do with the substitution of Roger Moore for Sean Connery as 007. Moore has the superficial attributes for the job: The urbanity, the quizzically raised eyebrow, the calm under fire and in bed. But Connery was always able to invest the role with a certain humor, a sense of its ridiculousness. Moore has been supplied with a lot of double entendres and double takes, but he doesn't seem to get the joke.' Years later, Ebert would recycle exactly the same line when The Living Daylights came out and say that Timothy Dalton didn't get the joke. You could maybe understand saying this about Dalton but not Roger Moore!

There was a better review from The New York Times, who wrote - 'Roger Moore is a handsome, suave, somewhat phlegmatic James Bond—with a tendency to throw away his throwaway quips as the minor embarrassments that, alas, they usually are. As Solitaire, to whom the cards speak truth only so long as she remains a virgin, Jane Seymour is beautiful enough, but too submissive even for this scale of fantasy. Yaphet Kotto (Dr. Kananha), a most agreeable actor, simply does not project evil. However, I could list compensating virtues by the score. There is a marvellous escape from an alligator farm (deadly reptiles are rather a motif in this movie), a superb collection of grotesque ways of killing, and a fine sense of pace and rhythm. Live and Let Die has been especially well photographed and edited, and it makes clever and extensive use of its good title song, by Paul and Linda McCartney.'

Variety seemed to find the film decent enough - although not vintage Bond. 'Live and Let Die, the eighth Cubby Broccoli-Harry Saltzman film based on Ian Fleming's James Bond, introduces Roger Moore as an okay replacement for Sean Connery. The script reveals that plot lines have descended further to the level of the old Saturday afternoon serial. The comic book plot meanders through a series of hardware production numbers. These include some voodoo ceremonies; a hilarious airplane-vs-auto pursuit scene; a double-decker bus escape from motorcycles and police cars; and a climactic inland waterway powerboat chase. Killer sharks, poisonous snakes and man-eating crocodiles also fail to deter Bond from his mission.'

By the way, many years later Live and Let Die also got a computer game in 1988. After their disastrous A View To A Kill game, Domark bravely ventured back into the world of Bond games with Live and Let Die. A game based on Live and Let Die sounds sounds great right? Well, don't get your hopes up too much. For one thing this game didn't even begin life as a Bond game. It was supposed to be a boat chase game called Aquablasters and a follow-up to Buggy Boy. Domark simply bought the game and slapped Live and Let Die on top of it. I suppose they figured that as the film Live and Let Die has a lengthy boat chase sequence, Aquablasters, with a few modifications, would make a good adaptation.

Domark's Live and Let Die is very forgettable on the whole. It's just a bog standard racing game only on water rather than a road. This is the sort of thing you would have bought if it was a budget title and then played for a few hours and completely forgot about. The most disappointing thing about the game is that it only consists of boat racing and makes no attempt to incorporate other aspects of the film. Live and Let Die is not the worst game ever made but it is very average and a fairly lazy sort of licenced game. By the way, the rendition of the 007 theme in this game is absolutely dreadful!

Roger Moore's debut movie Live and Let Die grossed $161.8 million from a $7 million budget. $161.8 million from 1973 in today's money would be blockbuster territory. EON could breathe a sigh of relief. Live and Let Die was a hit and audiences seemed to accept Roger in the part much more readily than they did George Lazenby. While the reviews were somewhat all over the place and critics (predictably and in rather tiresome fashion) sometimes unfavourably compared Roger to Sean Connery, the Bond franchise had managed to relaunch itself successfully. At this point the chances of Roger making the three films he was contracted to seemed pretty good.

Roger's first film outside of the Bond franchise was 1974's Gold. Gold is a romantic/adventure/thriller/disaster film based on a novel by Wilbur Smith. Some old hands from the Bond stable were onboard to to lend their experience to Gold. Peter Hunt (director of On Her Majesty's Secret Service) helms while Maurice Binder adds a very Bondesque title sequence. John Glen, who served as editor, second-unit director and full-fledged director during his long association with the Bond series, supervised some of the mine flooding sequences in Gold. Gold is one of the better non-007 films Roger featured in and some notable veterans were roped into proceedings with John Gielgud and Ray Milland taking supporting roles. Susannah York is the love interest for Rog while Bradford Dillman and Tony Beckley are wonderfully nasty as the villains.

The acclaimed composer Elmer Bernstein scored Gold and earned an Oscar nomination with Don Black for the song Wherever Love Takes Me. The film, somewhat controversially, was made in South Africa although some of the mine sequences were created using sets at Pinewood. Gold wasn't too much of a stretch for Roger Moore, given that he plays the stalwart hero, but he was certainly enjoying the chance to make movies again after his years as Simon Templar on the small screen. It wasn't all plain sailing for Rog and his career though. In his memoir he said he had courted the part of the assassin in the 1973 film the Day of the Jackal but the director Fred Zinnemann snubbed him and cast Edward Fox instead. Zinnemann said that he didn't want a famous actor to play the enigmatic assassin and this was why he had passed on Roger Moore.

Little time was wasted on moving ahead with the next Bond film. The Man With the Golden Gun was next to be adapted and arrived in 1974 - only a year after Live and Let Die. This was the film that Cubby and Harry previously had vague plans to make in the late 1960s with Roger. These days it takes several frustrating years for a new Bond film to come out so it is pretty remarkable to think that there was a time when you got Bond films in consecutive years!

The Man with the Golden Gun is the thirteenth James Bond novel written by Ian Fleming and was first published, posthumously, in 1965. The book begins with Bond - who was missing presumed dead because of the events of You Only Live Twice where he ended the story suffering from amnesia after an epic final encounter with Blofeld - turning up in London again and being granted an audience with M. However, during the meeting, Bond begins to rabidly extol the benefits and superiority of communism and then attempts to murder M with a stream of liquid cyanide. He is foiled and apprehended and it transpires that 007 had been brainwashed by the Russians in Vladivostok - a place he had gone to seeking to unlock something about his past.

Bond is duly deprogrammed and restored to something resembling his old self by electroshock therapy. Retirement seems the most likely option for our troubled hero but M decides instead to give Bond a new - and quite possibly last - mission. Bond is asked to travel to the Caribbean to terminate Francisco "Pistols" Scaramanga, a legendary killer known as "The Man with the Golden Gun" for his chosen instrument of choice, a gold-plated Colt 45. The feared Scaramanga is backed by Cuba and is known to be responsible for the deaths of several British agents. If Bond succeeds he can perhaps be of use to Queen and Country again, if he fails he will become Scaramanga's latest and most famous victim

Generally regarded to be one of the weaker, if not the outright weakest, of the James Bond novels, The Man With the Golden Gun has a slightly experimental feel and a somewhat unfinished air, almost as if it was accidentally printed just before the final conclusive draft was completed. Apparently Kingsley Amis, who penned the excellent Bond continuation novel Colonel Sun, gave the book a quick polish after Fleming died - with this unsurprisingly leading to enduring speculation about how much of The Man With the Golden Gun Fleming did or did not actually write himself.

One salient problem many had with the novel was the way that, brainwashed Bond angle swiftly dispensed with, it quickly returns to business as usual and gives Bond a small-scale adventure that seems anti-climatic after the epic and surreal events of You Only Live Twice. Though daft, the brainwashed Bond intro is very gripping and good stuff. As ever, the film would bear only a passing resemblance to the book save for character names and certain situations. The Man with the Golden Gun saw the same team who made the previous two pictures back again. Tom Manciwiecz would once again be penning the Bondian quips while Guy Hamilton signed up to direct his third Bond film on the bounce.

Manciwiecz apparently fell out with Guy Hamilton on this picture though and Bond veteran Richard Maibaum came back to finish the script. Richard Maibaum was critical of Live and Let - which he wasn't involved in - because he felt that a 'drugs in the jungle caper' was not a Bond plot. Guy Hamilton would later say that he personally regretted coming back to make The Man with the Golden Gun because he was bereft of ideas. Also bereft of ideas was the composer. John Barry didn't care much for his score for The Man with the Golden Gun. "It's the one I hate most ... it just never happened for me."

Jack Palance was approached to play Scaramanga in The Man with the Golden Gun but he wasn't interested enough to pursue the role. The part eventually went to horror icon Christopher Lee. This was apt because Lee was a cousin of Ian Fleming and used to play golf with the late Bond author. Two Swedish actresses, Maud Adams and Britt Eklund, were hired to play the female leads - Andrea Anders and Mary Goodnight. Eklund originally tested to play Anders but was then assigned the larger role of Mary Goodnight.

Maud Adams had only made a couple of films at the time but Eklund was very well known thanks to her marriage to Peter Sellers and she'd also been in films like Get Carter, The Night They Raided Minsky's, The Wicker Man, and Asylum. Cubby Broccoli thought Britt Ekland was too thin so before shooting began he took her to a lot of Italian restaurants to try and fatten her up and gain a few more curves. "To do a Bond film had been a dream for me," said Eklund. "It was the most glamorous and exciting time I have ever had on a movie. It does not make any difference whether you are a good actress." Desmond Llewelyn was thankfully back as Q while Clifton

James, more questionably, was also back as Sheriff J.W. Pepper.

The French actor Hervé Villechaize was cast as Nick Nack - the diminutive sidekick to Christopher Lee's villain. Villechaize was later best known for the television show Fantasy Island. He, sadly, had a rather unhappy life by all accounts. Villechaize suffered from 'dwarfism' and near the end of his life his health was failing just as he was going through a difficult time in private. He shot himself in 1993 at the age of 50. His suicide message included the following line - '3am I can't miss with a dum dum bullet - Ha! Ha! Never one knew my pain - for 40 years - or more. Have to do it outside less mess.'

There were plans for David Hedison to return as Felix Leiter in The Man with the Golden Gun but they couldn't find a way to write Leiter into the story. Roger Moore said that when he made Live and Let Die it was obvious to him that the relationship between Cubby Broccoli and Harry Saltzman was strained and probably not destined to last for much longer. This indeed turned out to be the case. Harry Saltzman, who was in financial difficulties, left the Bond franchise in 1974 after The Man with the Golden Gun. He later sold his 50% stake in James Bond to United Artists.

Saltzman is widely believed to have assumed that the Bond franchise was on its last legs anyway and wouldn't go on for much longer. Cubby Broccoli retained the other 50% and became the solo producer on the Bond movies from The Spy Who Loved Me onwards. Although the relationship between Cubby Broccoli and Harry Saltzman was difficult (mostly thanks to Saltzman's original plan to sell his stake to the rival company Columbia Pictures) when their Bond partnership ended, several years later Cubby invited Harry to the premiere of For Your Eyes Only to show there were no hard feelings. The Man with the Golden Gun was truly the end of an era. It was the last Cubby/Harry 007 production.

Lulu was hired to sing the title song - though the result was not one of the very best Bond themes. "I think mine was probably the worst one ever," said Lulu years later. "Mine was not a great song." Alice Cooper also recorded a potential theme for the movie but was rejected in favour of Lulu. "It actually came in a day too late," said Cooper in 2011. "By the time [the producers] heard it, they'd already signed for Lulu's song. I went, 'You're gonna take Lulu over this? 'Cause it was perfect for The Man With the Golden Gun'.

We went to every single one of those John Barry albums to try and invent the perfect James Bond song, and even Christopher Lee, who played Scaramanga in the movie, said, 'Oh, man, why did we take the Lulu song? This song is the one!'" You can listen to Alice Cooper's Golden Gun theme on YouTube if you are curious. I find it a bit of a racket myself! It wasn't much of an improvement - if any at all - on Lulu's song.

Thailand was a primary location for the movie and there was also a trip to Hong Kong - where Cubby Broccoli came up with the idea for the wreck of the RMS Queen Elizabeth to be a secret MI6 base. Thailand was chosen as one of the locations after a production designer saw spectacular photographs of Phuket bay in a magazine. The association with Bond would make this part of Thailand a popular tourist attraction in the decades to come. For the 360 degree Barrel Roll car stunt over the bendy bridge in The Man With The Golden Gun, the car had to be driven at 39.5 and 40.5 mph and the placement had to be within 2 inches or else it all would all have gone horribly wrong.

Roger Moore didn't like the scene in The Man with the Golden Gun where Bond roughs up Maud Adams. He also didn't like the scene where Bond pushes the kid in the water either. There seems to be an attempt in The Man With The Golden Gun to toughen Moore's Bond up a bit and it is doubtful that this tactic works. It would probably be fair to say that Roger Moore would finally hit his stride and cement himself as Bond in The Spy Who Loved Me. The Man with the Golden Gun tries to make Roger behave like Connery or Lazenby's Bond in places and it just doesn't suit him.

The Man With The Golden Gun was released in 1974 when the energy crisis was headline news. Talk about circuitous! We seem to living in something of an energy crisis again these days. The plot of The Man With The Golden Gun involves Francisco Scaramanga (Christopher Lee), a refined and expensive 'Hitman' with a big reputation. Scaramanga is especially famous for using a 'Golden Gun' to kill his victims. He sends MI6 in London a golden bullet with the numbers '007' engraved on it. It's a clear message that he intends to kill James Bond next. Bond had been on the trail of a 'Solex Agitator' - a gadget that can harness the power of the sun, but is now ordered to take some leave lest he should be killed by Scaramanga. Bond being Bond though, he decides that he will go and find this Scaramanga character first. Soon, 007 is playing a deadly game of wits with both the 'Solex' and his own life at stake.

The Man With The Golden Gun follows on in the manner of previous entry Live And Let Die. It's fairly lightish in tone with a creeping emphasis on humour and visual jokes. One could certainly argue that some of the chase scenes in Roger's films got a bit slapsticky at times. It's a tricky thing in a Bond film to balance the story, action, and humour perfectly. The Man With The Golden Gun was moved quickly into production in a move intended to help establish Roger as James Bond to audiences (who were probably still wondering when Sean Connery was going to return).

The Man With The Golden Gun tends to rank near the bottom of many best James Bond film lists but I think this is unfair. It's certainly not vintage Bond or classic Bond but The Man With The Golden Gun is a classier and more entertaining film than a lot of people have given it credit for over the years. It lacks the scope of some other films in the series bond is saddled with a topical plot device which dates it somewhat but The Man With The Golden Gun is a colourful and likable enough addition to the series and has a certain amount going for it.

The film has a strange pre-credit sequence that is very interesting because it is SO strange. A stereotypical Mafia type character arrives on Scaramanga's private Island in the Far East. He appears to have been hired by Scaramanga's diminutive manservant Nick Nack to kill his boss, but all is not what it seems. The Hitman is there to give Scaramanga a bit of target practice in his funfair style 'Hall Of Mirrors'. The bright colours and visuals in these scenes look great. It's all very strange and entertaining although for the second film in a row Bond doesn't really feature in the pre-credit sequence.

Maurice Binder's titles are not his best ever and John Barry later confessed that Lulu's song was one of the weakest Bond themes for him. Personally, I think the song is reasonably catchy and camp in a seventies James Bond film sort of way and have never had a major problem with it. The majority of the film is set in Hong Kong and the Far East and The Man With The Golden Gun can be praised for its atmosphere and colourful sense of location. It never quite pays off its fascinating premise (the deadly battle of wits between Bond and Scaramanga) but it does have a lot going for it.

There's a fantastic car chase scene which builds up to an amazing 'spiral' car stunt involving the fragments of a 'bendy' bridge. The slide whistle sound effect which caps this sequence is often criticised for being unnecessary and silly but who cares? It's a Bond film! There is a very well done fight scene between Bond and some heavies in a belly dancer club in Beirut. Roger Moore has a funny quip at the end of this scene and writer Tom Mankiewicz gives Bond some decent lines throughout the film. Mankiewicz said that Roger Moore knew his way around a comedy moment or scene better than Connery so they upped the jokes. The moment where Bond asks why anyone would have a motive to kill him is good fun. "Jealous husbands!" replies M. "Outraged chefs! Humiliated tailors! The list is endless!"

Popular criticisms of The Man With The Golden Gun are usually aimed at the increasing slapstick humour and innuendo. Clifton James returns as Sheriff J.W. Pepper and is soon embroiled in comic capers involving elephants and falling into a river and later we get kung-fu schoolgirls. One could argue that these elements could all have been happily jettisoned from the picture. The film perhaps also lacks the huge grand scale set-pieces that you would usually expect from a James Bond film. A few more cliffhanger type situations world have been helpful.

It has to be said that Britt Ekland as Mary Goodnight ranks fairly high on Most Annoying Bond Girl lists. To be fair she isn't helped by the way her character is written but she does look good in a bikini! The biggest thing the film has going for it is the late great Christopher Lee as Scaramanga. Lee is excellent in the film and appears to have relished the chance to be a Bond villain and escape from a Dracula set for a few months. He's set up as the 'flipside' of Bond.

Both Bond and Scaramanga are killers, both are refined, but one works for his government and one is a free agent who works for himself. Scaramanga is eager to discuss this theme with Bond in the film and Roger Moore and Lee have some decent exchanges and scenes together. "At a million dollars a contract I can afford to, Mr Bond," says Scaramanga after Bond comments that he lives very well. "You work for peanuts, a hearty well done from Her Majesty the Queen and a pittance of a pension. Apart from that we are the same."

Hervé Villechaize as Nick Nack is a strange piece of casting that just about works. It was a nice twist on the hulking 'Oddjob' type assistant/henchman. Maud Adams as fine as Andrea Anders and adds a classy presence to the film. Bernard Lee and Lois Maxwell are of course in the film as M and Moneypenny respectively and Desmond Llewelyn makes a welcome return as Q after missing out on Live and Let Die. And, thankfully, The Man With The Golden Gun is also aided by the return of John Barry, the composer who always most seemed to fit the cinematic James Bond.

Barry's score in this film is not regarded as his best ever but it's pretty good. One other thing that should be mentioned in any review of The Man With The Golden Gun is the wreck of the RMS Queen Elizabeth in Hong Kong harbour which is used as a secret HQ for MI6 in the film. This topsy turvey location with slanted rooms is a nice offbeat touch and adds to the slightly strange atmosphere of the film.

Roger is still not quite settled on the best way to play James Bond in The Man With The Golden Gun. There is a moment in the film where he smacks Maud Adams around to get some information and it really doesn't suit his interpretation of Bond. His third film was the one where he finally established himself in the role and seemed to find the right balance to suit his own persona. On the whole though Moore is very polished and competent in the film and although a departure from the Connery/Lazenby model he managed to grow into the role and prove that different actors could keep it going.

The Man With The Golden Gun is entertaining although the pace does slacken now and again. It's not a lavish action-fest like some of the other Bond films but compensates with a good sense of atmosphere. Scenes in real locations like a kick-boxing fight add a nice air of authenticity to the film. The climax on Scaramanga's private island is good fun with solar guns, liquid helium pools, and some crisp banter between Bond and Scaramanga. The palpable weirdness that sometimes infests the first two Roger Moore films is a strength.

The Man With The Golden Gun is a colourful and slightly underrated addition to the 007 series but it isn't a spectacular film likely to win the Bond franchise many converts. I suspect that the poor reputation of The Man With The Golden Gun both at the time and these days is a consequence of the fact that the film seems a trifle low-key and dull compared to the (spectacular) likes of Goldfinger and You Only Live Twice. I quite like The Man With The Golden Gun myself but can understand the perception that it is a Bond film which never really gets out of second gear. The film also fails to play to Roger Moore's strengths but Roger would be much better served in the next picture. It seems that Roger was much more in sync with Lewis Gilbert than Guy Hamilton and the evidence for this would be forthcoming in 1977.

CHAPTER FIVE- THE SPY WHO LOVED ME

The Man With The Golden Gun premiered at the Odeon Leicester Square in London on 19 December 1974. Prince Philip was the guest of honour. It would be fair to say that The Man With The Golden Gun met with a very tepid - even hostile at times - reception from critics. Most of the critics seemed to find The Man With The Golden Gun a rather uninspired and tedious film and, even with general audiences, it did not generate the curiosity and excitement of Roger's debut the year before.

Writing in Time magazine, Jack Cocks savaged the film with little mercy. 'Roger Moore, who first played 007 in Live and Let Die, lacks all Connery's strengths and has several deep deficiencies. He has all the worldliness of a floorwalker, and looks as if his last adventure was spending two weeks in a Swiss clinic getting a facelift. Although the final screen credits promise that Bond will return in The Spy Who Loved Me, it is time to retire him. He should be packed off to a sanatorium, where he can give his liver a rest and wait in leisure for his moment to come again. Right now, Bond has been around too long to be fresh, but not long enough to qualify as a genuine antique.'

The New York Times was equally unenthusiastic and also, rather unfairly, went out of its way to compare Roger to Sean Connery. 'Whether Mr Moore is twisting a woman's arm to discover a fact that he already knows, or nuzzling an abdomen without enthusiasm, he merely makes you miss his predecessor. The only energetic moments are provided by Herve Villechaize, as a midget gifted with mocking authority, and Christopher Lee as the golden gunman—both have a sinister vitality that cuts through the narrative dough. The movie also includes some beautiful glimpses of Thailand. But if you enjoyed the early Bond films as much as I did, you'd better skip this one.'

The Observer in Britain also gave The Man With The Golden Gun a big thumbs-down. 'This series, which has been scraping the bottom of the barrel for some time, is now through the bottom with depressing borrowings from Hong Kong kung fu movies, not to mention even more depressing echoes of the Carry On smut.' The Sunday Telegraph was also very unimpressed. "There seems to have been hardly and attempt to interest us in characterisation, least of all with Roger Moore - who plays Agent 007 with a negative kind of smug roguishness" You could add Variety to the negative critical chorus too. 'Guy Hamilton's direction and the screenplay are comparatively placid and even monotone. At this rate, the tenth film might be phoned in.'

It wasn't all doom and gloom though. The Mirror newspapers in Britain praised both the film and Roger Moore and Judith Crist of New York Magazine called the film entertaining and stylish. Generally though, it was a very bumpy critical ride for The Man With The Golden Gun. EON would definitely have to up their game if the Bond franchise was going to continue. There was a strong sense that The Man With The Golden Gun was a lacklustre by the numbers entry which hadn't got the best out of Roger Moore. Roger shouldn't be slapping women around in his Bond movies. That was simply making him play against type and needlessly drawing unnecessary comparisons to Sean Connery.

The lacklustre aura of The Man With The Golden Gun was illustrated by its poster art - which came across as a lazy rehash of the Live and Let Die posters. There were a number of commercial tie-ins with the movie - including toys, and deals with Nikon, Faberge, cigarette lighter brands, and more besides. It was to no avail though as The Man With The Golden Gun was a box-office disappointment. The film grossed $97.6 million from a $7 million budget. This was considerably down on Live and Let Die and the North American box-office (where The Man with the Golden got a severe mauling from The Godfather: Part II and Young Frankenstein) in particular was fairly dismal.

Roger Moore could be forgiven at this point for wondering if his assumption that he'd only make a couple of Bond films before it fizzled out might actually come to pass. Back in 1974 things were not looking terribly good at all for the Bond franchise. With the departure of Harry Saltzman it would now be up to Cubby Broccoli alone to refloat the sinking franchise. The legal complications arising from Harry Saltzman getting out of the Bond racket and selling his stake meant there was a three year gap before the next film came out. These days that seems like no time at all (modern Bond fans would consider it a miracle to get a new film only three years after the previous one!) but back in the seventies it was considered unusual to have to wait this long for the next film.

In a way this gap was necessary and good because the next Bond film had to be planned carefully. It had to be extra special. It couldn't just be business as usual. The Bond franchise, if it was going to survive the decade and beyond, had to find a way to be a big deal again. The next picture would have to be an extravaganza capable of wowing audiences and perhaps even critics too. With no Bond film on the immediate horizon, Roger Moore continued to work - although the results at this time were patchy to say the least and even slightly eccentric.

After finishing The Man with the Golden Gun, Roger was eager to stay busy and agreed to make a romantic comedy called That Lucky Touch for producer Dimitri de Grunwald. Roger's main reason for signing was the chance to work with Sophia Loren - who was slated to play opposite him as the female lead. Unfortunately for Roger, Dimitri de Grunwald couldn't get Loren and they only found out she wasn't going to do it with two weeks left until shooting commenced. Roger suggested his Gold co-star Susannah York instead and all agreed so York replaced the missing Sophia Loren. The film was made in Belgium and Roger enjoyed his time there with co-stars like Shelley Winters. The film was not a success though and has been practically forgotten today.

While Roger waited for production to start on the next Bond movie he kept as busy as he could and even took a role in the Italian exploitation crime action film Gli esecutori (aka Street People, The Executors) for producers Manolo Bolognini and Luigi Borghese. It seems rather strange that the current James Bond would be in a film like this but then, to be fair to Roger, his then wife was Italian and the chance to spend some time in Rome probably seemed like a good idea. Also, he would starring alongside the respected American actor Stacy Keach. Street People was not much of a success and remains arguably the most obscure film of Roger's career.

Roger had better luck with the 1976 film Shout at the Devil. Shout At the Devil saw Roger working again with director Peter Hunt and producer Michael Klinger to adapt another Wilbur Smith novel. A number of capable hands from the James Bond films added their expertise besides Hunt. Maurice Binder, Derek Meddings, John Glen etc. The film is based (loosely) on the sinking of the SMS Königsberg. Shout at the Devil was the most expensive film made in 1976, costing around $9,000,000. Michael Klinger again provoked controversy by shooting in South Africa with South African finance.

The headline star besides Roger was Lee Marvin. Roger seems to like Marvin in his memoirs but does say that the American actor was frequently drunk on the set. When they did the fight scene Roger writes that Marvin was drunk and - with a red mist in his eyes - threw punches for real! Shout At the Devil wasn't marketed very well in North America and so was somewhat underexposed there but it has held up fairly well over the years and is generally regarded to a decent old-fashioned period action film with some nice production values and special effects.

The last thing Roger did before returning to Bondage was to play the lead in the television film Sherlock Holmes in New York. This television film was not based on any of the literary stories but rather a new screenplay involving Holmes written

by Alvin Sapinsley. The director was the experienced Boris
Sagal, a man who had credits on many shows. The Twilight
Zone, Alfred Hitchcock Presents, Columbo, Peter Gunn, The
Man from U.N.C.L.E, amongst others. Sherlock Holmes in
New York has a mixed reputation amongst Holmes enthusiasts
but Roger enjoyed making it a great deal as he got to spend
some time with co-stars Patrick Macnee and John Huston.

The credits at the end of The Man with the Golden Gun
promised that The Spy Who Loved Me would be the next film.
The Spy Who Loved Me was the tenth Bond novel by Ian
Fleming and published in 1962. Fleming didn't care much for
it himself and gave instructions that only the title was to be
used in any film version and - generally - The Spy Who Loved
Me is not regarded to be one of the best books in the series. It
does have fans though and the rather polarising nature is
probably best explained by this being a different type of Bond
book that found Fleming in experimental mood.

In The Spy Who Loved Me, Fleming departs from his usual
structure and the story is told first person by his heroine
Vivienne Michel. Vivienne is a French-Canadian on the run
from an unhappy and complicated past who ends up at a
lonely job at the Dreamy Pines Motor Court, a motel in the
remote Adirondacks. While a storm rattles outside, Vivienne
has to close the motel down and look after the place but she
ends up in big trouble when a pair of criminals named Sol
'Horror' Horowitz and Sluggsy Morant turn up with orders by
their boss Mr Sanguinetti to burn the place down for insurance
purposes. Vivienne is beaten and held hostage and things look
rather bleak. Until that is a mysterious man with a flat tyre on
his car suddenly turns up at the motel. His name is James
Bond.

When he wrote the book Fleming was apparently becoming
slightly tired of churning out Bond novels and wanted to tinker
with his formula. Fleming didn't like the idea that the Bond
books were seen merely as entertaining pot boiler thrillers and
was seeking a bit more critical recognition for his literary

endeavours. It takes quite a while for anything of note to happen in The Spy Who Loved Me but there is tension generated when the villains show up and Bond arrives. The backstory of Vivienne does flesh her out as a character and make us feel like we know her quite well. Even by Fleming standards, this entry is quite sadistic at times with Vivienne taking a battering from Sol and Sluggsy.

The atmosphere of the novel - remote mountainous location, the telephone is out, wild storm etc - is nicely conveyed. These are not your typical Bond villains but nasty all the same and somewhat grotesque in the Fleming fashion. Sluggsy has an absence of hair anywhere on his body and very bloodshot eyes and Sol 'Horror' has steel-capped teeth (clearly the inspiration for 'Jaws' in the completely different film version). Despite its flaws, Fleming's The Spy Who Loved Me is certainly an interesting and different sort of Bond yarn.

Before The Spy Who Loved Me came out in 1977, people were starting to wonder for the first time if James Bond had outstayed his welcome and that maybe the franchise should gracefully retire. The Man with the Golden Gun failed to do much for either the box-office or critics in 1974 and legal wrangles meant that for the first time ever there would be a three year gap in between films. Cubby Broccoli, in his usual fashion, decided that he was going to prove all the cynics and doomsayers wrong and restore James Bond to his former glory. That he did with one of the most absurdly fantastical, entertaining, and lavish adventures in the history of the franchise.

Cubby Broccoli hired numerous writers to have a bash at the script for The Spy Who Loved Me. They included John Landis, Anthony Burgess, and Stirling Silliphant. Multiple scripts were commissioned for The Spy Who Loved Me. In one of the drafts, the villain had a secret base at Loch Ness. The original concept for The Spy Who Loved Me's PTS was completely different and had Bond on a raft before surfing ashore.

Richard Maibaum's original screenplay opened with a group of terrorists, comprised of everyone from the Red Brigade to the Weathermen, breaking into an ultra-modern Spectre lair. "They level the place, kick Blofeld out, and take over," explained Maibaum. "They're a bunch of young idealists. In the end, Bond comes in and asks, 'All right, you're going to blow up the world. What do you want? ' They reply 'We don't want anything. We just want to start over—the world is lousy. We want to wipe it away and begin again. So, there's no way we can be bribed.'

Cubby Broccoli nixed the early Maibaum script treatment as he thought it was too political. Some of the script treatments for The Spy Who Loved Me featured Blofeld and SPECTRE but when Kevin McClory got wind of this he took legal action. McClory argued that his Thunderball rights meant that only he was allowed to use these Bond elements. Around this time Kevin McClory intended to produce an unofficial Bond film with his Thunderball rights which would have been called Warhead. In the unused screenplay/treatment - which McClory, Len Deighton and Sean Connery all worked on together - for Warhead, Shrublands was a scuba-diving training school for intelligence agents rather than a health farm and the story would have featured robotic sharks and Blofeld threatening to destroy New York. Strangely, the villain and aquatic elements of McClory's aborted film are similar to The Spy Who Loved Me.

In the end it was Christopher Wood and the reliable Richard Maibaum who were credited with the story for The Spy Who Loved Me. Christopher Wood, believe it or not, wrote the Confessions series of novels and films. These were saucy sex comedies with Robin Askwith. Wood later wrote the 1985 action film Remo Williams: The Adventure Begins for the director Guy Hamilton. Christopher Wood proved to be a good fit for the Roger Moore era of Bond. He also wrote the novelisations for The Spy Who Loved Me and Moonraker. Wood had strong views about Bond. In 2012, he said of the current Bond films - "I am not shaken and stirred by 'new'

Bond. The movies seem like imitations of the Bourne series and I find Daniel Craig, though a good actor, akin to a muscle-bound Hobbit. I miss the lightness of touch of the old Bonds and having shifted uneasily through Casino Royale was not tempted to see the next one."

Guy Hamilton was hired to direct The Spy Who Loved Me but left in the end to go and make Superman for the Salkinds. Hamilton eventually left Superman too though and was replaced by Richard Donner. Cubby Broccoli replaced Hamilton on The Spy Who Loved Me with another former Bond director - Lewis Gilbert. Gilbert had directed You Only Live Twice back in the 1960s. With respect to Guy Hamilton, The Spy Who Loved Me and Superman both ended up in the hands of someone who was better suited to the material. Lewis Gilbert knew how to make an old school popcorn Bond extravaganza with all the 007 cinematic bells and whistles and that was exactly what the new film needed to be.

Lewis Gilbert was also shrewd when it came to Roger Moore's version of Bond. Gilbert believed that the new movie had to play to Roger's strengths and not force him to mimic Sean Connery - as The Man with the Golden Gun had done in places. "In the first two films, said Gilbert, "the producers were still thinking of the Sean Bond. That's not Roger. What Roger had was something different. He wasn't as good as Sean in the most sadistic moments - when Sean killed someone you knew they were really dead. With Roger you somehow never quite believed it - but Roger was much nearer to the Bond in the books. He also bad his own kind of breeziness and charm, more in the David Niven manner."

The veteran German-Austrian actor Curd Jürgens was cast as the villain Stromberg on the suggestion of Lewis Gilbert. Gilbert had worked with him before on other films. Gilbert wanted a suave and composed villain and felt that Jürgens was perfect. Jürgens had made millions of films - which included Battle of Britain, The Longest Day, and The Inn of the Sixth Happiness. Curd Jürgens was also in OSS 117 – Double Agent with 'almost Bond' John Gavin. Horror fans might remember Curd Jürgens from the enjoyable Amicus anthology film Vault of Horror.

Tom Mankiewicz said that Catherine Deneuve wanted the part of Anya Amasova in The Spy Who Loved Me but negotiations broke down because Cubby Broccoli wasn't willing to pay the $250,000 she wanted to star in the film. Lois Chiles was also courted for the part but she told the producers she had retired from acting. Marthe Keller and Dominique Sanda were also considered but in the end Barbara Bach was given the part of Anya Amasova in The Spy Who Loved Me. Bach, a New York born model, was cast only days before the film began shooting. Bach didn't have many acting credits. She was in the 1971 giallo thriller Black Belly of the Tarantula (which featured Bond Girl Claudine Auger and unofficial Bond Girl Barbara Bouchet) and the 1968 miniseries Odissea. Bach seemed to mostly make films in Italy. She also appeared with Usula Andress in the 1973 film Motel of Fear.

Barbara Bach was, at the time, the girlfriend of United Artists Executive Danton Rissner. Rissner asked Cubby Broccoli if he could find her a small part in The Spy Who Loved Me and she ended up as the female lead. Rissner was said to be a bit shocked and nervous when he found out that Bach had been given such a large part! Bach wasn't the greatest actress in the world and the director Lewis Gilbert had to do multiple takes for some of her scenes in The Spy Who Loved Me. Bach didn't do too much acting after James Bond. In 1979 she appeared in the cheapjack Star Wars copycat The Humanoid with her Spy co-star Richard Kiel. Bach later married the Beatle Ringo Starr after meeting him on the set of the 1981 comedy film Caveman.

Caroline Munro was cast as Naomi in The Spy Who Loved Me after Cubby Broccoli saw her picture as part of the Lambs Navy Rum campaign. Munro was best known for her association with Hammer Horror films and had appeared in Dracula A.D. 1972 and Captain Kronos – Vampire Hunter. Her other credits included the two Dr Phibes films with Vincent Price and At the Earth's Core with Peter Cushing. Will Sampson was considered for the part of Jaws. Sampson was best known for his part as Chief Bromden in One Flew Over the Cuckoo's Nest. Jack O'Halloran (best known as the mute bearded Kryptonian villain Non in Superman II) turned down the part of Jaws before it went to Richard Kiel. David Prowse, the man in the Darth Vadar suit for the original Star Wars movies, was also considered for Jaws.

The 7 foot 2 inches tall Richard Kiel (his distinctive features and size were the result of a hormonal condition known as acromegaly) attributed his casting as the steel toothed henchman Jaws to a short lived television series called Barbary Coast, a sort of sequel to Wild Wild West (where Richard had also played a baddie). A casting director saw Kiel in the series and suggested to Cubby Broccoli that the towering actor would be perfect for Jaws. In Christopher Wood's novelisation of the film The Spy Who Loved Me, the real name of Jaws is Zbigniew Krycsiwiki. Milton Reid, who played Sandor (the fellow Bond holds up by his tie before dropping him from the buiding) in The Spy Who Loved Me, was previously in contention to play Oddjob in Goldfinger. Reid was also in the first Bond movie as one of Dr No's guards.

A surprising guest star in The Spy Who Loved Me is Michael Billington - who could easily have been playing Bond in the movie had things turned out slightly different back in 1972. Billington has a small role as the doomed Soviet agent Sergei in the PTS of The Spy Who Loved Me. Billington's role as Sergei is the closest we ever got to seeing him as Bond - although he said that he did not play the character in the same way he would have played 007. "I knew that if I did it, it might prevent me from doing Bond in the long run," said Billington, "but I thought "Why not?" A couple of weeks skiing and Bond was only a picture or two from demise anyway, or so I thought. What did I care? My choice was should I try and play it like Bond? I decided to go the anti hero route, darker inside." Billington actually looks a lot like George Lazenby in the The

Spy Who Loved Me PTS!

Victor Tourjansky was the bemused onlooker in three Roger Moore films. Tourjansky was the man with the bottle on the beach when the Lotus comes out the water in The Spy Who Loved Me, the man with bttle (again) in Moonraker, and then the man with the wine glass surprised by the ski chase in For Your Eyes Only. Tourjansky was an Italian born second assistant director and writer. You can only really imagine these comic cameos happening in the Roger Moore era. When Bond's Lotus comes out of the sea onto a beach in The Spy Who Loved Me, Bond hands a fish to a bemused onlooker before he drives off. Cubby Broccoli didn't like the fish joke (he wondered how a fish would get in a waterproof underwater car!) and wanted it removed but Lewis Gilbert and Roger Moore both loved it and persuaded Cubby to let it remain the film.

Don McLaughlan, the head of public relations at Lotus Cars, used an ingenious but simple ploy to get the Lotus in the Bond films. He simply parked a prototype Lotus Esprit at Pinewood Studios! Someone from EON saw the car and the Lotus ended up in The Spy Who Loved Me. When the Lotus comes out of the water onto the beach in The Spy Who Loved Me, the car was secretly pulled by a rope to achieve the effect of it driving out of the sea. The car they used wasn't watertight either so Roger Moore and Barbara Bach got their feet wet shooting this scene. The little boy who points at Bond's Lotus as it drives out of the sea in The Spy Who Loved Me is Richard Kiel's son.

Cubby Broccoli built the largest soundstage in the world at Pinewood to make The Spy Who Loved Me. A huge space was needed for the supertanker interiors. Stanley Kubrick secretly helped with the lighting for the supertanker scenes in The Spy Who Loved Me. Kubrick did this as a favour to Bond's production designer Ken Adam. Bond model miniature maestro Derek Meddings said it was tricky to make the Liparus tanker model in The Spy Who Loved Me seem convincing. "The reason we built it so large was because we had to deal with submarines in the same shots. Water is always a problem when you're dealing with miniatures because you just can't scale it, you've got to be clever enough to shoot it the right way at a very high speed.

"The secret is to make certain you don't create a splash which is, of course, going to produce big globules of water on the screen and immediately give the game away. Even though our tanker was sixty-three feet long, it would only create a bow wave and wash that was in scale with a sixty-three-foot launch, which is nothing like what a supertanker with its vast displacement of water would create. Only the aft section was actually built like a boat, the rest was like a catamaran built on two floats. We had a huge 175 horsepower marlin engine in it which gave us a terrific wake though, of course, nothing near a real tankers."

Cameraman and professional skier Willy Bogner, Jr. was the man responsible for the amazing ski sequences in On Her Majesty's Secret Service, The Spy Who Loved Me, and For Your Eyes Only. Bogner was especially good at capturing footage while skiing backwards! Rick Sylvester, who performed the ski jump in the PTS of The Spy Who Loved Me, said that when he went to a preview screening he heard a member of the audience say to the person next to them that it must have been a dummy or mannequin that went off the mountain because no one could possibly have done that stunt in real life!

During production on The Spy Who Loved Me in Egypt, the crew were said to be in low spirits because of the heat and poor quality of the food. Cubby Broccoli therefore had his favourite pasta and tomatoes flown in, took over a local restaurant, and cooked spaghetti bolognese for the entire cast and crew. This raised morale and made Cubby even more popular. The Egyptian government assigned an official to the production whose job it was to make sure that nothing in the movie or script was at all derogatory about their country. Bond's wisecrack in the film about "Egyptian builders" was therefore dubbed in much later in the safety of Pinewood Studios thousands of miles away.

When he was interviewed on the set of The Spy Who Loved Me for the BBC, Roger Moore admitted that he didn't have the faintest idea what the plot of the film was! Roger had a bout of shingles shooting The Spy Who Loved Me. Shingles is a viral infection that causes a painful rash. Moore had a puffy face at one point (during the briefing scene with George Baker) and so they had to shoot a scene over his shoulder and avoid close-ups. Roger seemed happy and relaxed on the set of the film. This picture would mark the end of his Bond contract. He had no idea if he'd be in the next one - or if there would even be another Bond film. It would all depend on how successful The Spy Who Loved Me was. Trivia - On this picture, Roger Moore was the first Bond actor to shoot a second gunbarrel intro. He had to do this because of an aspect ratio change.

One important ingredient to the usual Bond stew would sadly be missing though on The Spy Who Loved Me. The legendary John Barry was living abroad for tax reasons and couldn't set foot in Britain without coughing up a very large sum of money to Her Majesty's Government so a new composer was needed. Who to choose? Step forward Marvin Hamlisch - the first American to ever be asked to compose a Bond score. Hamlisch was rather young at the time but had a very interesting background. His first stage work involved playing piano for an eightysomething Groucho Marx at Carnegie Hall. Hamlisch also scored two very early Woody Allen films (Take the Money and Run & Bananas) and went on to compose the soundtracks for The Way We Were and The Sting.

The Spy Who Loved Me was sort of like a fresh start for the Bond series. Make or break. It had to go for broke. The approach by Hamlisch to the music was to partly embrace the disco era and a more modern sound but also stay true to the John Barry template with majestic strings, brass and melodies. The title theme Nobody Does It Better is one of the most instantly recognisable and classic Bond songs. It was composed by Hamlisch and performed by Carly Simon (with lyrics by Hamlisch's girlfriend at the time Carole Bayer Sager). This is a very simple cheesy song, a big camp power ballad that is enjoyably melodic and somehow perfectly captures the seventies Roger Moore era.

Nobody Does It Better is like a masterclass in how to come up with a James Bond theme. It feels lavish, grand, and yet faintly tongue-in-cheek. The lyrics are simultaneously both rubbish and brilliant (it's something of a tradition that Bond lyrics don't always make an awful lot of sense if you actually sit down and study them!) and Carly Simon provides a nice vocal. Bond songs never quite feel right unless they are sung by a woman and this is certainly one of the more memorable ones.

So, was The Spy Who Loved Me good enough to save the Bond franchise? Was it the audience pleasing extravaganza the franchise needed? In a word, yes! Undersea bases, supertankers that swallow nuclear submarines, Richard Kiel with steel teeth, Union Jack parachutes. The Spy Who Loved Me makes Skyfall look like some student film made in a garage over weekends. The Spy Who Loved Me cost twice as much as any previous Bond and the money is up on the screen. It feels like a big and ambitious film compared to many previous - and subsequent - Bond entries. Cubby Broccoli spared no expense with the special-effects and spectacular locations - which include Sardinia, Egypt and Austria. Baffin Island in Canada was used for the pre-credit ski sequence and the Bahamas was used for key underwater scenes.

The film opens with probably the most famous and iconic stunt in Bond history. After a fantastic ski chase with funky music by Marvin Hamlisch, 007 (in a banana yellow jumpsuit) skis off a mountain top cliff and seems to fall forever before a Union Jack parachute opens. They thought they had actually missed the stunt (by Rick Sylvester) through technical problems with the various cameras but one camera managed to capture everything and a shaft of sunlight at the right moment, which seems to illuminate Bond as he reaches the edge, made it all almost too good to be true. The amazing stunt is an audacious start to The Spy Who Loved Me and an early sign that Cubby Broccoli meant business after being written off in the wake of The Man with the Golden Gun and Harry Saltzman's departure.

The confident beginning is continued by Maurice Binder's excellent pre-credit sequence and theme Nobody Does It Better, sung by Carly Simon. Both continue the impression that everyone has worked extra hard to make The Spy Who Loved Me special and not just another Bond film. The sequence at the start of the PTS onboard a British nuclear submarine is also well done and reasonably tense. The Spy Who Loved Me, in the best tradition of James Bond films, features a megalomaniac with a grand-scheme to alter the planet. Stromberg (Curd Jürgens) is a potty shipping tycoon who has been capturing nuclear submarines using a gigantic supertanker! He also has an undersea base called Atlantis which majestically rises from the sea like a giant spider as he listens to classical music.

The futuristic Atlantis and production design give the film a sci-fi feel much more in the spirit of the gilt-edged sixties Bonds like You Only Live Twice - whose plot is borrowed here. Atlantis and the hijacking of the nuclear submarines are superbly realised by the model work of Derek Meddings. I am often nostalgic for the days before CGI when models ruled the world of film and FX and The Spy Who Loved is great fun for this reason alone. Stromberg wants the nuclear missiles from the submarines to destroy the human race and build a new future for mankind under the sea.

Jürgens is nicely deadpan as Stromberg and has some good lines; "Farewell, Mr Bond. That word has, I must admit, a welcome ring of permanence about it." Sadly for him, he's made a big mistake by hijacking a Royal Navy submarine. This means that James Bond 007, in the suave guise of Roger Moore in a pair of cream flares, is sent to investigate by the British government. Moore is soon dispensing quips and throwing people off roofs in Egypt before straightening his tie in his usual unflappable style.

The humour in Spy is up on previous Bond films and Roger seems much more at home than in his previous entries - where he was still required to play against his personality a little. Moore was lighter in tone than the other Bonds but provides a suave, funny and - amidst great mayhem and silliness at times - commanding presence throughout the film. Roger seems to have a better grasp here of when to play it straight and when to wink at the audience - in contrast to his first couple of 007 adventures.

After a vague but obvious attempt in Live and Let Die and Golden Gun to avoid comparisons with Connery by stressing Bondian traits, Moore is seen in Naval Uniform here and a reference to his (Bond's) dead wife is made. The Spy Who Loved Me explicitly states that Roger Moore IS James Bond and feels much more Bondian and cinematic than Roger's first two adventures. Bond has to team up with Soviet Agent 'XXX' Major Anya Amasova, played by Barbara Bach, after they cross swords both chasing a vital submarine tracking system. The chase takes them to the pyramids where they first meet Henchman for hire, and killer, Jaws, played by the 7ft 2 Richard Kiel.

Jaws' indestructibility is used for a lot of jokes, Kiel often dusting himself down and walking off with a stoic expression after crashing his car through someone's roof or being thrown out of a moving train! Jaws sums up the comic book and sci-fi themes running through the film. The Spy Who Loved Me's funky seventies feel and lavish production design make a winning combination for me. With the exception of Oddjob, Jaws is definitely the most iconic and memorable henchman that Bond has ever tangled with.

The photography is superb and it's great fun to see Roger walking around in the desert in a tuxedo. Barbara Bach, a bit like Jane Seymour in Live and Let Die, is not the world's greatest actress but is one of the more beautiful Bond ladies, not least walking around the pyramids in a slinky black dress. There is a dramatic subplot where XXX finds out that Bond killed her lover during the (pre-credit) ski-chase and promises to kill him when the mission is over but it never quite works because Bach isn't very convincing and Roger's Bond doesn't seem like the stressful type anyway!

XXX and 007 do have amusing moments of one-upmanship as they work together. After another classic Roger Moore Bond train punch-up, this time with Jaws, Bond literally being pinned to the ceiling before deploying electrical sparks from a lamp on Jaws' metal teeth!, 007 and XXX investigate Stromberg's Sardinian base. This section of the film is about as much fun as a Bond film can get. Bond receives his iconic seventies white Lotus Esprit and has a typical encounter with Q. "Now I want you to take good care of this equipment." "Have I ever let you down, Q?" "Frequently!"

Bond poses as marine biologist Robert Sterling and is allowed to meet Stromberg on Atlantis. Jürgens and Moore are really good fun together in this scene. Back on dry-land Bond and XXX return to Q's gadget-laden Lotus Esprit and, in a fantastic chase sequence that lasts for ages, survive numerous attempts on their life by explosive motor-cycle side-cars, gunmen and a helicopter! Roger Moore is in his element here, dispensing quips and deadpan looks at Caroline Munro's seductive helicopter pilot as she tries to kill them.

There is some great model work with lorries exploding and the chase between the Lotus and helicopter is amazing. Most people remember this film as the one with the underwater car. This is superbly done (by Meddings again) and leads to another action sequence underwater! The music by Marvin Hamlisch for this sequence is great fun. Hamlisch wisely came up with some action cues of his own and avoids overdoing the James Bond theme. The Sardinia section really highlights the intention and spirit of The Spy Who Loved Me.

The climax of The Spy Who Loved Me features a spectacular battle scene in the submarine dock located within Stromberg's supertanker as the submarine crews are released and fight a battle against Stromberg's men. The return to grand production design and over the top sets pays dividends and the technical complexity of shooting such an action-packed scene is well handled by Lewis Gilbert. The final encounter between Bond and Jaws is memorably funny too; "How does that grab you?"

How would one describe The Spy Who Loved Me? Colourful, fantastical, and action-packed. It's the best of the Bond films that Roger Moore starred in, the mixture of humour and technological escapism striking a better balance than some other slightly silly entries in the series. The Spy Who Loved Me is carried off with considerable panache and style and is as grandly entertaining as any film in the long running series. Cubby Broccoli pulled out all the stops on Spy and it really shows. If you simply want to have fun and don't mind some fantastical trappings in your Bond movies then The Spy Who Loved Me is absolutely brilliant.

CHAPTER SIX - MOONRAKER

The Spy Who Loved Me had a sun drenched Royal Premiere at the Odeon Leicester Square in London on 7 July 1977. The date read - 07/07/77. Her Royal Highness Princess Anne was the guest of honour. It is said that the audience cheered and applauded when Bond's Union Jack parachute opened after his spectacular leap off the mountain ledge in the PTS. A few months earlier Roger Moore and Barbara Bach attended the Cannes Film Festival to promote the forthcoming film. The marketing was much more lavish than it had been for The Man with the Golden Gun and, boosted perhaps by the three year gap (which made this Bond movie more of an event), The Spy Who Loved Me made James Bond feel like big news again.

One amazing success in the marketing was the return of Corgi Bond models and the Lotus in particular was a huge seller. United Artists spent (a then incredible) $4 million marketing The Spy Who Loved Me. This movie was make or break for the Bond franchise so no stone was left unturned in making sure it was a success. The Intercontinental Hotel in Park Lane was hired by Cubby Broccoli for a lavish party after the premiere.

The reviews for The Spy Who Loved Me were, happily, much improved from The Man with the Golden Gun. 'From the opening credits to the final fade-out kiss the latest James Bond epic is unqualified joy,' wrote the Daily Mirror. 'This is cinema entertainment at its very best.' The Sun was equally enthused and wrote - 'It is the best Bond film so far. The sexiest, the fastest-moving and certainly the most witty.' TIME magazine praised aspects of the film but also argued that the plot and Bond formula was mechanical. They loved the opening stunt though. 'They'll never top first stunt: skier hurtles off precipice. Long breathtaking plunge. Shucks off skis in midair, free-falls for a while, then opens parachute and floats earthward. Wow.'

The Los Angeles times was also complimentary. 'The Spy Who Loved Me is an extravagant silliness, a high-cost undertaking in let's pretend which delivers a perfect formula. It may not be everyone's tonic, but it is what it says it is, rousingly.' Newsweek was also won over and opined - 'After the opening sequence, much of the action in The Spy Who Loved Me, the tenth James Bond screen epic and the third starring Roger Moore as Bond, is somewhat downhill. But the film, shot in seven countries, is so rich in fantasy, so filled with beautiful scenery, gorgeous women, preposterous villains and impossible situations that's it easier to suspend disbelief entirely and escape inside the gadgetry and glamour.' Northwest Herald felt that the film was "Not only Roger Moore's best, but one of the few Bond films that can stand apart from the series as a superb action movie."

There were, unavoidably, still some sniffy notices though from the more grouchy critics. The Washington post suggested that - 'The Bond movies have been so successful that it may be commercially impossible to terminate the series. However, it's been quite a while since a Bond adventure appeared to set fashions in escapist, glamorous entertainment. Once widely imitated and parodied by other producers, Bond films are now more likely to imitate themselves with decreasing effectiveness.'

Variety was also determined to be sniffy and wrote - 'As always, story and plastic character are in the service of comic strip parody, an excuse to star the prop department, set designer, stunt arrangers, the optical illusion chaps, and such commercial suppliers as the maker of the sporty Lotus car, a lethal job that also converts to an underwater craft.' The New York Times was also rather on the grumpy side and wrote - 'During the course of The Spy Who Loved Me, James Bond vanquishes an amphibious building that looks like a giant spider, a 7 foot 2 inch villain with metal fangs, hundreds of hapless extras and one very beautiful broad, but he hardly ever comes to grips with his most insidious adversary, the James Bond formula.'

It had cost nearly twice the budget of The Man with the

Golden Gun to produce and The Spy Who Loved Me was - to the delight of Cubby Broccoli's bank manager you'd imagine - a huge box-office success, grossing $185.4 million. This was double what Golden Gun had made. The film broke box-office records in several countries and was so popular in Britain that it played in some cinemas until after Christmas!

United artists and EON were thrilled to see too that The Spy Who Loved Me did very well in the United States. Cubby Broccoli could breathe a heavy sigh of relief. He had not only proved that Bond was still a viable commodity going forward he had also proved that he was more than capable of producing these films alone. The Spy Who Loved Me's positive reception and financial success was just reward for the effort Cubby had put into this pivotal movie.

Cubby Broccoli already had plans to adapt For Your Eyes Only as the next movie. Roger Moore's three film contract had expired with The Spy Who Loved Me but Roger told Cubby he would be perfectly willing to do a fourth picture. Cubby was more than happy to keep Roger in place. The Spy Who Loved Me had cemented Roger Moore as James Bond in a way that Live and Let Die and Golden Gun hadn't. The Spy Who Loved Me was truly Roger Moore at the height of his powers as Bond. He looks terrific in the film and his performance is confident and witty. Although the action, mayhem, and gadgets were all greatly heightened in The Spy Who Loved Me and it is an overtly fantastical film, Moore's charisma is always sufficient to keep his head above water.

There was a strange coda at this time when Gerry Anderson threatened legal action after The Spy Who Loved Me came out because he claimed it bore similarities to a Moonraker treatment he had written for Harry Saltzman several years previously. Anderson was persuaded to drop his case in the end. The Moonraker script treatment that Gerry Anderson and Tony Barwick wrote for Harry Saltzman in the early 1970s had a villain named Zodiac and identical triplet henchmen. Zodiac was hijacking nuclear submarines in the story so you can probably see why Anderson threatened legal action when 1977's the Spy Who Loved Me came out.

Many years later in 1990 there was a computer game based on The Spy Who Loved Me. This game was by Domark - who by now had mastered the art of making disappointing James Bond games. The Spy Who Loved Me appeared on various platforms - most notably the Amiga. It got a PC release but didn't sell very well. A game based on The Spy Who Loved Me sounds like an exciting prospect on the face of it. You might be expecting a ski sequence or a section set around pyramids. You don't get any of that in the end. About 90% of this game is basically a remake of Spy Hunter. Spy Hunter was a good little game for its day but you'd expect an Amiga game to be a lot more ambitious than that.

The Spy Who Loved Me begins with a terrible rendition of the Bond theme and a gunbarrel featuring a blocky spirited figure who bears no resemblance whatsoever to Roger Moore. The first section involves Bond and Anya in Sardinia driving to the hotel. Bond's car is obviously his gadget equipped Lotus. This is a top down driving section where you have to dodge pedestrians and pick up Q tokens which are scattered in the road at various points.

The game doesn't let you go to the next level unless you pick up enough Q tokens so you you have to make slow progress to ensure that you don't just drive past them. After a few minutes of this the level quickly becomes tedious. The next level of the game is a top down speedboat section. You have to avoid swimmers, pick up more tokens, and use missiles to shoot enemies. You must also use ramps to jump over obstacles. What any of this has to do with The Spy Who Love Me I don't know. It's suddenly more like a Live and Let Die game. This speedboat section, like the first driving section, soon becomes monotonous.

There is another driving section next in Sardinia again. This time there are enemies trying to force you off the road and you have to drive into a Q truck at various points to get more equipment. You get some gadgets like missiles and the ability to spray paint at enemy cars. While this might sound exciting it isn't much fun to play. Once again you have to pick up those tokens (which are becoming annoying by now) because you won't be able to progress in the game if you don't get enough of them.

The second Sardinia section goes on for far too long and becomes very repetitive. The missiles you fire are weedy and poorly animated and in no time at all you want the level to end so you can move onto something else. The objective is reach the jetty so that the Lotus can dive off into the water. It is a great relief when this finally happens. The next level is the underwater Lotus section. At last we have something different. This level looks good and is a welcome relief after that endless driving section.

The underwater Lotus is equipped with missiles and must fight frogmen and mini submarines. I like the bubbles that come out the back of your Lotus. This level has more zip to it than the car driving section (which is strange as it takes place underwater) and the weapons and combat is punchier and more satisfying. The Spy Who Loved Me becomes a vertically scrolling shooter in the underwater section and that's a good thing as far as I'm concerned because I was getting awfully tired of the Spy Hunter style levels.

At the end of this level you have to destroy a giant structure armed with powerful lasers. By this stage the game has become considerably more difficult but I'm not complaining because the shoot 'em up action has at least given us more entertainment than the early levels ever provided. The next level takes place on Stromberg's supertanker. You have to attack the control room. There's quite a nice backdrop here with a captured submarine laying in the water.

This supertanker level mixes up the gameplay again. It is an Operation Wolf/Cabal style shooting gallery level. The 'shooting gallery' type of game was briefly popular around this time but rendered completely obsolete in the end by the FPS genre. Why would you play Cabal anymore when you can play Doom? You use the mouse in the control room section to move a cursor around and shoot both frogmen and Stromberg's men running around platforms. Once you've done this you have to alter the launch codes of Stromberg's missiles. The next level has Bond riding a jetski and firing missiles at boats and speedboats. The level is basically a vertically scrolling shooter style of game again. It isn't as much fun as the underwater car section but it at least has some zip and speed to it and there is plenty of action.

The final level is another Operation Wolf style shooting gallery and takes place in a corridor on Stromberg's undersea base Atlantis. You have to shoot red boiler suited goons and Jaws makes an appearance - which is nice. Stromberg also makes an appearance with Anya as a hostage. Anya looks nothing like Barbara Bach and is wearing a bikini that leaves little to the imagination. This last level is fiddly and difficult to the point of being unfair. You might need cheat codes to get through it.

The game ends with an image of Bond and Anya in the escape pod. Once again the likeness to Roger Moore is atrocious. The Spy Who Loved Me was Domark's last Bond game but sadly it isn't an improvement on the consistently mediocre list of Bond games which made up a fair portion of their back catalogue. Parts of the game are quite good but those Spy Hunter style sections are not very interesting at all and leave a poor impression. If you slog your way through the rest of the game (and good luck with that) you are at least rewarded with the decent underwater car level but those shooting gallery sections are nothing to write home about.

Roger Moore went straight back to work after The Spy Who Loved Me was completed and appeared in The Wild Geese - which was an action caper about veteran mercenaries on a dangerous African mission. The Wild Geese is the first and best known of the films that Roger Moore made with director

Andrew V McLaglen and was based on a novel called The Thin White Line by Daniel Carney. McLaglen had directed some lesser John Wayne westerns and was chosen when John Ford put in a good word for him with producer Euan Lloyd. Lloyd had resisted the suggestion by the studio that Michael Winner direct the film.

The Wild Geese is an all star war adventure film and fufilled Lloyd's ambition to make a Dirty Dozen style caper with many famous names in the cast. Burt Lancaster was set to star at one point but when he made one too many demands about his character and his fee he was replaced by Richard Harris. According to Roger, OJ Simpson was lined up to play his own part before he was cast! The film was made in South Africa and there were demonstrations by anti-apartheid campaigners when it was released.

In mitigation, the producers highlighted the positive response the film had received when it was shown in Soweto and the subplot where Hardy Krüger's bigoted white South African mercenary comes to respect the deposed black African leader he has to protect. Well, fair enough but there is no way to completely get around the fact that the villains to be mowed down in this war film are not Hitler's Nazis but black Africans. James Bond connections? Future Bond director John Glen edits while Syd Cain handles the production design. Maurice Binder supplied the very Bondesque titles for The Wild Geese.

Roger played ace pilot Lieutenant Shawn Fynn in The Wild Geese - a film that is much more violent than James Bond. It is sometimes said that Roger should have played Bond the way he did Shawn Fynn. Much of this I suspect comes from a scene early on when Fynn, while working as as a currency smuggler, forces a drug dealer to eat his own drugs. It's a pretty nasty scene and displays Roger in a much more cold and ruthless light than James Bond (save perhaps for the car kicking moment in For Your Eyes Only). But Roger is not entirely convincing dispensing some rough justice to drug pushers. His main strengths lay in light comedy and being debonair.

Roger's next movie was Escape to Athena, which was another war picture for Roger during his stint as James Bond - this time a World War 2 caper that makes a vague attempt to be The Great Escape but ends up playing more like Hogan's Heroes on a bigger budget. Producer Lew Grade assembled an enviable cast for the picture besides Roger. David Niven, Richard Roundtree, Telly Savalas, Claudia Cardinale, Elliott Gould etc. Grade felt the film was ultimately too much of a mish-mash that couldn't decide if it was a comedy or an action film. He felt it should have concentrated on the action.

Despite bad reviews, Escape to Athena didn't lose as much money as Grade had feared. Roger plays (don't laugh) Major Otto Hecht, the commandant of a POW camp for Allied soldiers in the Mediterranean. He felt (as he usually did) that he was miscast and this time he may have been right. Call me cynical but I think the location shoot on the Greek island of Rhodes might have had something to do with Roger's decision to make the film! If nothing else it was probably a very nice holiday.

Meanwhile, back at EON HQ, Cubby Broccoli had changed his mind about For Your Eyes Only being the next Bond film and decided that Moonraker would be the next picture. Moonraker was the third James Bond novel in the series of books written by Ian Fleming and originally published in 1955. The story revolves around a mysterious tycoon called Sir Hugo Drax. Drax, in a move regarded as an altruistic gesture to the British Government, is the driving force behind a nuclear missile project called 'Moonraker' which he is developing in Kent near the coast. The revolutionary missile contains top secret elements that only Drax controls. It will safeguard the security of Britain in the unstable and uncertain era of the cold war.

When M, the head of the British Secret Service - MI6 - discovers that Drax may be cheating at Bridge, in M's club Blades of all places, he asks James Bond to go and confirm or deny his suspicions by gambling with Drax. Bond lays a trap and discovers that Drax is indeed cheating. But why? He's a millionaire building a top secret weapon for the government. Can he be trusted? When a government official assigned to Drax's Moonraker project is killed, M decides that James Bond must travel to the Kent coast and unravel the mystery of Hugo Drax once and for all. Moonraker picks up the pace when Bond travels to Romney Marsh to investigate the Moonraker Project and more specifically Drax. He meets Gala Brand there. Brand is undercover investigating Drax for Scotland Yard and she teams up with Bond to unravel the secret of the Moonraker project.

As usual, the film made by EON, save for a title and character names, would bear little resemblance to Fleming's novel. Moonraker is often tagged as EON's attempt to latch onto the Star Wars craze but you could argue that the movie is often more influenced by Kubrick's 2001 than Star Wars. Nonetheless, the incredible success of Star Wars in 1977 was clearly the main catalyst for Cubby deciding to send Bond into space.

Lewis Gilbert was signed to direct again and Christopher Wood wrote the screenplay. The obvious tactic of Cubby Broccoli was simply to keep The Spy Who Loved Me team in place. If it isn't broke why fix it? Tom Mankiewicz previously wrote an unused script treatment for Moonraker for EON and Mankiewicz's treatment included elements which were used in later Bond films. These most saliently included an Acrostar jet chase (which was used in Octopussy) and an action setpiece in Paris (A View To A Kill).

Moonraker ended up costing well over thirty million dollars to make. This dwarfed even the budget for The Spy Who Loved Me. The eighties Bond films later had increasingly static budgets because they were still paying off the interest on Moonraker going over budget. John Glen complained that the static budgets of the Bond films made it difficult to stage all the action in Licence To Kill. Moonraker was so expensive that EON and MGM were still having to instigate an austerity drive to pay for it ten years later!

James Mason was supposed to play Hugo Drax in Moonraker but because the production was moved to Paris (due to high tax rates in Britain at the time) a quota of French actors had to be cast and so Michael Lonsdale got the part of Drax instead. Lonsdale had been appearing in films in his native France since 1956. The suave Louis Jourdan had been approached for Drax but he wasn't interested. Jordan would of course though later play a villain in a Roger Moore Bond film. Lino Ventura and Stewart Granger were also considered for the part of Drax. The stipulation that Moonraker had to contain a certain number of French actors helped Corinne Cléry bag the part of Corinne Dufour.

Jaclyn Smith was the first choice for the role of Holly Goodhead in Moonraker but she couldn't do it in the end because of a production clash with her television show Charlie's Angels. This paved the way for Lois Chiles, now apparently unretired, to play the part. Chiles had appeared in films like The Great Gatsby, The Way We Were, Coma, and Death on the Nile. She was not only beautiful but also a very competent actress so one can see why EON were so keen on her. Chiles said her character was not a 'dingbat' but an equal of Bond. She said she quite enjoyed having a stereotypically risque double-entendre Bond character name in the film! Legend has it that Lois Chiles ended up in Moonraker after - purely by chance - sitting next to Lewis Gilbert on a plane.

Due to his popularity in The Spy Who Loved Me, Richard Kiel was asked to return as Jaws. Two different endings for the Jaws character were shot for Spy and they went for the one where he emerges from the water after the tussle with the shark to live another day. Blanche Ravalec was cast as Jaws' girlfriend Dolly. Drax's henchman Chang was played by Michael G Wilson's aikido instructor Toshiro Suga and Lois Maxwell's daughter plays one of the 'perfect specimens' Drax has collected. Sadly, Moonraker marked the last appearance of Benard Lee as M.

The Bond team took over the biggest soundstages in Paris to

shoot Moonraker - much to the annoyance of the local film industry. Roger Moore said he loved making Moonraker in Paris because the relaxed French crew didn't start work until noon! During the production of Moonraker in Paris, the French actress Carole Bouquet visited the set. Bouquet obviously made a big impression on Cubby Broccoli because he cast her in the next movie - For Your Eyes Only. The door code to the bio-room in Moonraker is the theme from Close Encounters of the Third Kind. Steven Spielberg had to be asked permission to use this. In return, Spielberg was allowed to use the James Bond theme in The Goonies several years later.

The PTS freefall in Moonraker required over 90 jumps before sufficient footage was in the can. The parachutists could only film very limited footage on each jump. You could argue that Roger Moore's finest hour as Bond comes in Moonraker when Bond emerges from the centrifuge and looks genuinely rattled. To achieve the rippled effect on Bond's face from the G-forces, high-pressure hoses were rigged to blow at Roger's face.

It was very difficult to shoot the gondola sequence in Moonraker because Venice was full of tourists and they kept rushing up to take photographs of Roger Moore and the Bond production. In the end, the production had to come up with a diversion in which they would pretend to be shooting in one location and attract crowds while the REAl shooting went on somewhere else. The Venice section took about three weeks to shoot and was hindered by heavy rain. All in all, the Venice section was something of a nightmare to get in the can.

Happily, John Barry was back to score Moonraker. It's one of Barry's greatest scores and deserves to be ranked alongside his very best work on the franchise. Moonraker marked a slight change of direction for Barry away from strident brass more towards lush orchestration and strings and was in many ways the template for all the films he would subsequently score in the 1980s. His Moonraker soundtrack is bold, brave, ambient and absolutely wonderful at times. Never has the sound of

James Bond been quite so dreamy and lavish.

Kate Bush was approached to sing the theme song for Moonraker but declined because she was about to go on tour and simply didn't have the time. It was eventually Shirley Bassey who sang the theme - marking the third time she had done this. The title song Moonraker has Barry and Shirley Bassey back together one more time and is an affecting enough ballad that certainly sounds very James Bondian. This is a slower one but very melodramatic and wonderfully composed. Strangely, Bassey was only a last minute replacement for Johnny Mathis - who bailed when he decided he didn't like the song!

Roger's appearances as James Bond after The Spy Who Loved Me were negotiated on a film by film basis. Roger and Cubby Broccoli would basically play a game of bluff with one another before each film. Roger felt he wasn't paid enough and Cubby thought he was asking for too much. Despite these divergent positions though the two always remained friends and always seemed to manage to strike a last minute deal for Roger to come back.

Though Roger Moore was no spring chicken in the last phase of his tenure as Bond (Roger was already in his fifties by the time he made Moonraker) he was popular with audiences (ignore lazy retrospective articles which try and tell you that Roger Moore was hopeless as Bond - he was terrific and impossibly made the part his own after Connery) and pleasant and professional to work with. For this reason EON were reluctant to part company with Roger. Roger was also a great Ambassador for the franchise and never put a foot wrong in interviews. He was a classy and funny frontman for the Bond machine.

There were though, given Roger's age and film by film arrangement, plenty of potential Bonds waiting in the wings during his era in case he didn't come back. In fact, Cubby would often openly test actors as a way to put pressure on

Roger to make a decision. The suave English actor Michael York wrote in his autobiography that after the financial success of the 1976 sci-fi film Logan's Run he was approached by Cubby Broccoli and asked if he would be interested in playing James Bond. York said that while he was flattered he didn't think he was right for Bond. It appears that Cubby was sounding out potential Bond candidates from the mid to late seventies onwards - lest his film by film arrangement with Roger Moore should run into obstacles.

Patrick Mower claims that after Roger's third Bond (The Spy Who Loved Me) he was brought in to do an audition because Cubby wasn't sure that Roger would be back. "They thought he was too old to do another three films and he hadn't signed his contract," said Mower. "So they tested me again. But then Roger signed his contract." Around this time Mower was appearing in the cheapjack and largely forgotten police television show Target. He would surely have loved nothing more than to land James Bond.

Michael Billington was also still very much in the loop. When EON were testing actresses for Moonraker, Michael Billington was brought in to play Bond in the auditions against prospective leading ladies. "I got the call to go to Paris for another series of tests. Moonraker was being 'Prepped' and they were looking at Bond Girls. I didn't feel much like playing Bond having just played a crazed underworld criminal but I took the job. I did some scenes with imported beauties like Shelly Hack and Susan Reed. Also local talent such as the beautiful Sylvia Krystel and a lovely girl called Cyrielle Besnard."

Billington said that, after the auditions, the director Lewis Gilbert told him he should play James Bond in the next picture. Billington was invited to dinner with Cubby Broccoli after the auditions and had become close to Cubby's young daughter Barbara. It seemed that Michael Billington was still very much in pole position to be the next Bond. He was essentially sitting on the substitute's bench waiting to be called onto the pitch at any moment.

Moonraker is certainly one of the most distinctive films in the Bond series. Some people love it and some people hate it. It's fair to say that Moonraker is definitely not one for Bond purists who like a bit of grit with their Bond film! Ian Fleming's excellent Moonraker novel with its elaborate card-game and Bond's investigation of the mysterious Hugo Drax on the Kent coast was deemed unusable except for the title and a few names and set-pieces. Instead, Cubby Broccoli set out to make the biggest and silliest Bond film ever.

In the film Hugo Drax, much like Stromberg, wants to destroy the human-race and start again. Drax plans to create a race of super humans in space to take over the Earth. The film opens with the RAF flying a Moonraker space shuttle over Britain. Security must have been a bit lax because two rascals are hidden in the shuttle. They start the engines up and steal the shuttle, destroying the 747 that was carrying it.

M asks where 007 is. Moneypenny tells him that 007 is on his last leg and he is, quite literally. At this point you can probably guess that Moonraker isn't going to be the most realistic stab at James Bond. Roger Moore, in a cream polo-neck and blue blazer is thrown out of an aeroplane with no parachute. He steals one in mid air and finds that Jaws is after him in, er, mid air. Is this entertaining and fun? Well, to be honest, yes it is!

Bond is sent to investigate Drax in California. He is flown over the tycoon's property in a helicopter to the strains of John Barry's music and I'm completely unapologetic about liking Moonraker for a reason that this scene illustrates: Moonraker seems like a really, really, really big film. And a stylish one too. After Bond has met Holly Goodhead (Lois Chiles) and made a 1970's sexist remark "You're Dr Goodhead? A WOMAN?" he meets Drax. Michael Lonsdale is dryer than a cream cracker with nothing on it in Moonraker and seems to be having fun with his role.

Drax's henchman Chang (Toshiro Suga) tries to kill 007 in a centrifuge. This is possibly the best scene in the film and Ken Adam's set is absolutely amazing. Bond's face starts to ripple as the G-forces reach a dangerous level but he remembers his wrist activated dart gun, demonstrated on that horse's arse in M's office. 007 staggers from the cockpit and shrugs off Holly's attempts to help him. Is this moment Roger Moore's finest as Bond? It might be.

The trail leads Bond to Venice. "Ah Venice" as Indiana Jones might say. Pigeon double-takes and a gondola hovercraft. Well, this section does take 'comedy' Bond a bit too far (as we've noted, some of the chase sequences in Roger's films are a bit too long and slapsticky) but the punch up with Chang in the museum is a lot of fun and quite hard-hitting. Roger Moore is often branded Bond-lite but his scraps were always well staged and he was often a lot tougher than he is given credit for.

Bond investigates Drax's laboratory and discovers a toxic nerve agent under development but Drax erases all trace of the labs when Bond bursts in with M and the Minister of Defence. 007 looks rather foolish but has craftily maintained a vial to prove his theory and is ordered to Rio de Janeiro. In Rio de Janeiro, 007 is re-introduced to Jaws (who has been hired by Drax). I did enjoy the idea that Drax had to employ a new henchman after Chang was killed. I often wonder what Jaws does when the henchman sector slows down. Does he sell double-glazing? A side career in wallpaper? Jaws going through the airport metal-detectors is a funny gag.

The cable-car fight doesn't quite work but there is some incredible and very dangerous stuntwork in these scenes. Jaws meets Dolly and most Bond fans wish he hadn't. Holly is captured and 007 heads for Brazil dressed as Clint Eastwood. "Balls Q?" There is a running gag where Moneypenny doesn't believe Bond when he explains what has happened to him since he last saw her. It makes me chuckle anyway. Bond travels up the amazon in a speedboat searching for Drax's research facility and is predictably attacked by several other boats and Jaws. This is good fun although some poor back projection work surfaces in this scene. Back projection is a technique that hasn't aged well and it tends to blight a lot of old action and thriller films.

Some of Drax's perfect women entice Bond inside a jungle temple and after a fight with a rubber snake, 007 is reunited with Jaws and Drax. Drax's control room is another amazing set. Imagine what the The Crystal Maze would have looked like if it had a budget of $100 million an episode and was designed by Ken Adam! Well, that's Drax's control room.

Bond and Holly are tied in the blast pit underneath a shuttle about to take off. They escape and pose as pilots in a shuttle of their own. Derek Meddings terrific model work still holds up very well.

The final half hour in space sees the end of Drax and his space station and something that few people ever expected to see in a Bond film - a gigantic battle in space with lasers! Oh, and Jaws turns from villain to goodie. "I think he's attempting re-entry, sir!" says Q in the end. Your tolerance for all this depends on your weakness for just one sci-fi epic comic book Bond with a lot of comedy and a very seventies feel. I have no problem in admitting that I enjoy Moonraker on these terms although it is hard to think of anything more way out ever appearing again in the form of a James Bond film.

Moonraker has been much derided in the years since its release and to this day is often held up as as object lesson in how James Bond films can get out of control if you don't ration the humour. Many consider it to be the worst Bond film ever made but that's grossly unfair. If you removed Blanche Ravalec's Dolly from the story and edited some of the action (the back projection during the boat chase and cable car sequence is poor for such an expensive film) Moonraker has a lot going for it. It looks fantastic, has a great score, and even some tense scenes away from the comic hijinks.

Problems? The film is too long for its own good and the humour (most famously, a pigeon actually does a double-take when Bond takes to gondola hovercraft in Venice) is unrestrained at the best of times. The Jaws character is demystified here to the point where he loses all of his menace. A word too about the product placement, something which all Bond films have to incorporate to some degree but here, well, it just seems far too intrusive and obvious. Moonraker has the most shameless product placement scene in the history of the movie franchise when the ambulance navigates the hill and we see nothing but billboards in the background.

Overall though I'm always charmed by the boldness and spectacle of Moonraker. It has classic cinematic Bond moments like the centrifuge and Bond shooting the sniper in the tree, a great villain, some great lines ("Mr Bond, you defy all my attempts to plan an amusing death for you...", "You appear with the tedious inevitability of an unloved season..."), amazing production design and special-effects that still work today. If you can take it for what it is Moonraker is a fun way to spend a couple of hours.

CHAPTER SEVEN - FOR YOUR EYES ONLY

Moonraker had a lavish marketing campaign which included many space themed toys, an annual, and even a 007 bubble bath. Who wouldn't want some James Bond bubble bath? Roger Moore also fronted a television special too in order to promote the film. There was a lot of anticipation and hype for the film. Bond hadn't been this big a deal since Sean Connery was around. Moonraker premiered on 26 June 1979 at the Odeon Leicester Square in London. The Duke of Edinburgh, Prince Philip, was in attendance and celebrities included Britt Ekland, Joan Collins, Dodi Fayed, Dino De Laurentis, and Richard Johnson (the actor who famously turned down a contract to play James Bond in Dr No).

A bearded Roger Moore was also there along with many members of the cast and crew. Richard Kiel, an unmistakable figure for obvious reasons, was a big attraction at the premiere and seemed to be enjoying himself. The swanky afterparty was held at the London Playboy Club. In the preamble to the release of Moonraker, Roger Moore said "Cubby Broccoli hasn't asked me to do another, but then he never does until he sees how much money he makes from the last one I've done." Roger had negotiated a share of the gross for Moonraker. This turned out to be a shrewd deal because Moonraker set box-office records for Bond which stood until the Pierce Brosnan era. Adjusted for inflation, Moonraker was a blockbuster for its time.

The New York Times gave Moonraker a glowing review in 1979 when the film was released. 'At a time when everything is being either inflated or devalued it's comforting to know that at least one commodity maintains its hard currency. That's James Bond, who, by all rights, should be an antique, as emblematic of the 60's as the Beatles and flowerpower, but who goes blithely on as if time has had a stop. Moonraker, which opens today at the Rivoli and other theaters, is the 11th in the remarkable series that began in 1963 with Dr. No and it's one of the most buoyant Bond films of all. It looks as if it cost an unconscionable amount of money to make, though it has nothing on its mind except dizzying entertainment, which is not something to dismiss quickly in such a dreary, disappointing movie season. Almost everyone connected with the movie is in top form, even Mr. Moore who has a tendency to facetiousness when left to his own devices. Here he's as ageless, resourceful and graceful as the character he inhabits.'

The Globe and Mail was also impressed, writing - 'In the first few minutes – before the credits – it offers more thrills than most escapist movies provide in two hours. The excitement has gone all the way up to giddy and never comes down.' Time magazine was also kind to the film. 'If Moonraker is not quite as satisfying as Spy, the best of the post-Sean Connery Bonds, the difference is in the casting. Lonsdale is a bit too tame; he seems to be doing a John Ehrlichman imitation. Chiles is all too sexless. The title song, the important kickoff for Bond movies, is no match for Nobody Does It Better, the Carly Simon dazzler of Spy. Still, one does not tend to notice these failings as Moonraker unfolds. Broccoli just keeps piling on the goodies: lush Ken Adam sets, gadgetry and gams galore, super stunts and effects. It may be another two-year wait for the next Bond film, so you may as well just stuff yourself silly now.'

Variety was also reasonably kind to the film. 'Christopher Wood's script takes the characters exactly where they always go in a James Bond pic and the only question is whether the stunts and gadgets will live up to expectations. They do. The main problem this time is the outer-space setting which somehow dilutes the mammoth monstrosity that 007 must save the world from. One more big mothership hovering over earth becomes just another model intercut with elaborate interiors. The visual effects, stuntwork and other technical contributions all work together expertly to make the most preposterous notions believable. And Roger Moore, though still compared to Sean Connery, clearly has adapted the James

Bond character to himself and serves well as the wise-cracking, incredibly daring and irresistible hero.'

TIME was also rather kind to the film and wrote - 'Wood pulls off some witty flourishes. There are funny references to other blockbuster movies (Close Encounters, Superman, Sergio Leone westerns), as well as amusing bursts of comic-book dialogue. Rather than stage variations on Jaws' old fiendish gags, Wood has given the character some surprising twists, including a love interest. As always, there is no explicit gore or sex to jolt the audience back to reality. If Moonraker is not quite as satisfying as Spy, the best of the post-Sean Connery Bonds, the difference is in the casting. Lonsdale is a bit too tame; he seems to be doing a John Ehrlichman imitation. Chiles is all too sexless. The title song, the important kickoff for Bond movies, is no match for Nobody Does It Better, the Carly Simon dazzler of Spy. Still, one does not tend to notice these failings as Moonraker unfolds. Broccoli just keeps piling on the goodies: lush Ken Adam sets, gadgetry and gams galore, super stunts and effects. It may be another two-year wait for the next Bond film, so you may as well just stuff yourself silly now.'

Roger Ebert was a trifle grumpy though about Moonraker and didn't seem very impressed. He also, tediously, went out of his way to compare Roger Moore unfavourably to Sean Connery. Ebert's main complaint was that Moonraker was too fantastical and gadget festooned. 'The stars of this movie are Ken Adam, the art director, and Derek Meddings, in charge of special effects. In addition to the gigantic space station, they provide lots of little touches, like 007's gondola in Venice, which turns into a speedboat and then miraculously grows wheels. Moonraker is a movie by gadgeteers, for gadgeteers, about gadgeteers. Our age may be losing its faith in technology, but James Bond sure hasn't.'

There were certainly some negative reviews when it came to Moonraker. Many felt that the balance of himour, plot, and action in Moonraker had slid too far towards humour - to the point where the film was a parody of Bond. Richard Maibaum was among those who held this view. He felt Moonraker was too silly and thought Roger Moore had a tendency to spoof the part. Maibaum later said that the Bond series could do without what he called 'that space station crap'. This felt a trifle unfair because Roger did what he was given to play. If he was given a tense or 'straight' scene, like the centrifuge sequence, Roger was always terrific. There was definitely though a 'backlash' against the comic book sci-fi excesses and comedic nature of Moonraker in the end and this persuaded Cubby Broccoli that a course correction might be needed for the next picture.

One other person who also criticised the film was none other than Sean Connery. "I went in London to see Moonraker with Roger and I think it's departed so much from any sort of credence from the reality that we had [in my six films]," said Connery. "Such a dependence on the effects and there's no substance." I can't say that I agree with Sean that there was 'reality' in his Bond films. I love the Connery Bond films but you'd hardly call films like You Only Live Twice, Goldfinger, and Diamonds Are Forever realistic! There has never been a realistic Bond film. Even the famously 'gritty' Daniel Craig films are full of ridiculous implausible scenes.

When Moonraker was released in 1979, Gene Siskel in the Chicago Tribune took issue with the movie's gratuitous and gruesome product placement. 'In the beginning of the Bond series, before they were thought of as a series, each film was a good action picture with a colourful, entertaining hero. Today, they come off as conglomerate business enterprises rather than movies. How else does one explain the intrusive commercial plugs in Moonraker for Christian Dior perfume, British Airways, Bollinger champagne, Glaston boats, and Seiko watches? Truly, money derived from these plugs can't be worth the loss of story continuity when the products are flashed in front of the camera. Someone is being awfully cheap about the plugs, which borders on incredibility because the James Bond series is one of the surest moneymakers in the film business. Maybe the producers of Moonraker are blind to story construction?'

Siskel was right about Bond being a sure moneymaker because Moonraker grossed $210.3 million - which was even more impressive than The Spy Who Loved Me. The film was a global hit, breaking records in many nations. It had the widest ever American release for a United Artists film and drew record attendances in France. People in France were especially interested in Moonraker because it had obviously been an Anglo-French production.

While not everyone was happy about the direction in which the franchise was heading there was no doubt that it was, from a commercial standpoint, a popular and shrewd approach in the late 1970s. The problem was though that after Moonraker there was nowhere left to go with this Lewis Gilbert style fantastical approach to 007. EON would have to think very carefully about the tone and direction of the next film. They would also have to decide if they were going to carry on with Roger Moore.

There was a lot of doubt in the entertainment world in 1979 that Roger Moore would be back for a fifth film. Roger himself, as we noted, also seemed to cast doubt on his participation in the next picture. Roger was nearly 52 and although Moonraker was a big financial success there was a sense that the franchise could do with a change of direction and come back down to earth somewhat. The most logical way to do this was cast a new actor and begin a new era. This is essentially what EON planned to do at the time.

It was at the end of the seventies when Timothy Dalton got a brush with potential Bondage (if you'll pardon the expression). He was in his early thirties at the time. Dalton now seemed to be very much on the radar of Cubby Broccoli. Broccoli always kept a close eye on the male acting pool in Britain lest he should need a new Bond again. Timothy Dalton was someone that Broccoli always liked and had high up on his list of potential replacements for Roger. However, Timothy was apparently not that enthused by the prospect of playing James Bond at the time.

"There was a time in the late 1970s," Dalton later confessed in the book The Incredible World of 007, "when Roger may not have done another one, for whatever reason. They were looking around then, and I went to see Mr Broccoli in Los Angeles. At that time, they didn't have a script finished and also, the way the Bond movies had gone - although they were fun and entertaining - wasn't my idea of Bond movies. They had become a completely different entity. I know Roger, and think he does a fantastic job. He was brilliant. Roger is one of the only people in the world who can be fun in the midst of all that gadgetry. But the movies had gone a long way from their roots; they had drifted in a way that was chalk and cheese to Sean. But in truth my favourite Bond movies were always the first three."

While the Bond team worked out where to take the franchise next, Roger went back to work and appeared in four fairly movies soon after Moonraker. North Sea Hijack (also known as Ffolkes and Assault Force outside of Britain) saw Roger try to shake off his now firmly established James Bond image and play a very different type of character. This was probably too late as he'd been typecast since his Simon Templar days let alone James Bond but North Sea Hijack is an enjoyable little action/suspense yarn and Roger seems to be having fun. He plays an eccentric, grumpy and bearded marine counter-terrorist expert named Rufus Excalibur ffolkes (the small - and double - 'f' is no typo, it's an ancient English name apparently) who has a fondness for woolly jumpers, bobble hats, knitting, crossword puzzles and cats.

Rufus Excalibur ffolkes lives in a castle and drinks whisky from the bottle at a time when most of us are waking up with a mug of PG Tips. The film reunited Roger with Wild Geese director Andrew V McLaglen and the pair would soon work together again on The Sea Wolves. This is a slightly gentler affair than The Wild Geese but the villains are quite nasty and there are harpoon guns etc. It's not Mary Poppins. Roger has spoken of North Sea Hijack with some fondness. In his view he might have been somewhat miscast (I would disagree - Roger is great fun in the film) but he enjoyed playing the part of ffolkes. It made for a nice break from James Bond, especially after the long shoot on Moonraker.

A strong cast was assembled around Moore for North Sea Hijack with James Mason as Admiral Brindsen and Anthony Perkins and Michael Parks as the villains. Look out for George Baker and David Hedison too. Baker had appeared in On Her Majesty's Secret Service while Hedison played Felix Leiter in Live and Let Die alongside Roger several years previously. There was no escaping those Bond connections.

In 1980, Roger appeared in The Sea Wolves. The Sea Wolves reunited director Andrew V McLaglen, composer Roy Budd and Roger Moore with several cast members from The Wild Geese although sadly Richard Burton and Richard Harris are absent. Actors from The Guns of Navarone also feature - The Guns of Navarone in many ways the film that The Sea Wolves is trying to be. The screenplay is based on a real World War 2 operation that involved expatriate British veterans known as the Calcutta Light Horse Brigade undertaking a secret mission in Goa to disable transmissions being made to German U-Boats. The real life veterans are paid tribute to in the closing credits and we are also reminded that as a result of the Goa raid the amount of Allied shipping lost in the Indian Ocean fell dramatically.

The producer Euan Lloyd complained that The Sea Wolves wasn't marketed very well by the studio and it wasn't a tremendous success in the end. The most notable casting besides Roger was Gregory Peck as the lead and veterans David Niven and Trevor Howard. While The Sea Wolves is hardly the greatest war adventure film ever made it is at least pleasant to see all these famous names onscreen together.

In 1980, Roger also appeared in the Bryan Forbes segment of

the obscure anthology film Sunday Lovers. Sunday Lovers is another one of those films featuring Roger Moore that has largely been forgotten. This is a four segment comic anthology revolving around love and sex with four different directors involved. It seems somewhat reminiscent of Woody Allen's Everything You Always Wanted To Know About Sex (But Were Afraid To Ask) and even has a few actors from that film (Gene Wilder, Lynn Redgrave). Unfortunately, Sunday Lovers doesn't have Woody Allen's wit or comic flair and is a forgettable if not entirely uninteresting exercise. Roger, if his autobiography is anything to go by, seems to quite like his contribution segment to Sunday Lovers although he admits that the film never found an audience and didn't really click on the whole.

Roger's next film appearance was also something of a glorified cameo. The Cannonball Run was based on a real life outlawed road race (the Cannonball Baker Sea-To-Shining-Sea Memorial) that had already inspired two similar films in The Gumball Rally and Cannonball. It was directed by stuntman turned director Hal Needham. Needham had already directed a couple of films with Burt Reynolds, including Smokey and the Bandit. Reynolds, around this time one of the biggest box-office stars in the world, agreed to appear in the film as a favour to Needham. Reynolds picked up a multi-million dollar payday for a couple of weeks work and confessed later that he didn't like the film much.

The Cannonball Run is awash with famous faces and cameos although you may need to be American to recognise most of them. The really famous ones everyone will recognise? Rat Packers Dean Martin and Sammy Davis Jr, Burt and Dom DeLuise, Jackie Chan, Farrah Fawcett, and Roger sending up his Bond image and driving around in an Aston Martin. Roger explained in his autobiography that he told director Hal Needham that he wouldn't spoof Bond but he would spoof Roger Moore! So Roger plays a character who thinks he is Roger Moore - the actor who plays Bond. It was rumoured that Cubby Broccoli was unhappy at Roger's spoofery and made him sign a contract not to lampoon 007. Roger denied that this ever happened.

The Cannonball Run was lambasted by critics (especially Roger Ebert) but proved to be a big hit at the box-office and spawned a 1984 sequel. Roger declined to appear in the sequel because he felt the 'I am Roger Moore' joke had run its course in the first film and he'd also been upset by a car accident on the set that involved one of the women who played his companions. Stuntwoman Heidi Von Beltz was also left a quadriplegic after a terrible crash during the film.

The question now was whether or not we would see Roger back in the tuxedo and safari suit as Bond in For Your Eyes Only. This time the game of bluff between Roger and Cubby would go down to the wire. For Your Eyes Only is a collection of five James Bond short stories by Ian Fleming and was first published in 1960. Fleming had originally written the stories for a proposed series of Bond television adventures to be broadcast by CBS but that never transpired in the end. Two of the stories here were first published by Cosmopolitan and Playboy respectively. Although regarded to be an interesting offshoot from his series of Bond novels, For You Eyes Only is not generally regarded to be one of the strongest examples Fleming's work.

The first story is called From A View To A Kill and is set in and around Paris. Bond has to investigate the death of a motorcycle intelligence dispatch rider who was found in undergrowth with his important papers and documents missing. After studying the scene of the mystery, Bond decides to stake-out the area and discovers that Soviet agents are operating there from an underground base of operations. Despite the inevitable danger, he must infiltrate the group and expose the whole operation. From A View To A Kill, although a rather short story, takes a while to get going but Bond's investigation becomes more intriguing as it develops, especially when he uses camouflage to see exactly what is going on. This is an interesting but nothing special little story with Fleming's descriptive prose always enjoyable and a fun motorbike chase. At 37 pages though there is precious little time to flesh characters out or turn it into anything memorable.

The second story is called For Your Eyes Only. When Colonel Havelock and his wife are murdered, M, who was a guest at their wedding, sends James Bond to kill the culprits - who led by former Nazi war criminal von Hammerstein and had his men do it to get hold of the Havelock's property. Bond is sent on an ultra secret mission to Canada to complete his task but soon finds out that the Havelock's daughter, Judy Havelock, is out for revenge too. For Your Eyes Only, which contains strands and characters from the film that pilfered its title, is not bad with a range of far flung locations, a great scene between Bond and M - where M has a crisis of conscience over whether or not to have the assassins of the Havelock's killed - and an interesting political angle that was very topical when this collection was published. Hammerstein works for Cuban leader Fulgencio Batista who of course was deposed around this time. Hammerstein knows a big change is coming in Cuba and this has profound consequences for his choice of action. One could argue perhaps that Hammerstein is a little underdeveloped but his henchman Gonzales is rather nasty.

The third story is called Quantum of Solace. This has nothing whatsoever to do with the 2008 film of the same name and finds Bond enduring a dull dinner with the Governor of the Bahamas and guests in Nassau after his mission in Cuba. Things perk up though when the Governor tells Bond a tale about a governmental employee's relationship with an airline attendant, a dark and interesting story about human relationships that Bond finds fascinating, leaving him with much to muse on. This is a real departure for a Bond story but fascinating nonetheless with the story of infidelity and intrigue in Bermuda's British community always interesting - as too are Bond's reflections and thoughts. 'I should say you're absolutely right. Quantum of Solace - the amount of comfort. Yes, I suppose you can say that all love and friendship is based in the end on that.'

The fourth story is called Risico - which is one of the few
Fleming titles that EON have yet to pilfer for the film series -
and contains elements and characters that were later used in
the 1981 Roger Moore film For Your Eyes Only. This story
finds Bond travelling to various locations in Rome and Venice
to investigate a drugs smuggling ring and finding out that it is
sometimes difficult to work out who the real enemy is. This is
a decentish short story with intrigue and double crosses and a
couple of strong characters - Kristatos and Columbo - for Bond
to match wits with. Lisl Baum makes a memorable Bond
woman and there is an exciting raid on a warehouse that
makes for a good action set-piece. Risico perhaps takes a while
to get going but Fleming's descriptions of the locales are
enjoyable as usual although his attempts at regional lingo - 'In
this piznizz is much risico' - don't always work terribly well.

The final story is called The Hildebrand Rarity. While on
holiday in the Seychelles, Bond falls in with dubious
millionaire Milton Krest and is persuaded to join a search for a
rare spiked fish known as The Hildebrand Rarity which Krest
must find as part of a tax dodge. Krest beats his wife with a
whip and poisons countless fish looking for The Hildebrand
Rarity and the millionaire will be lucky to survive the boat trip
without getting his comeuppance. Possibly the most
accomplished story on offer here, The Hildebrand Rarity has a
rich exotic atmosphere that makes you feel as if you are on the
boat yourself in these languid and sun-drenched Indian Ocean
waters. There are great descriptions of the locations and the
underwater search too. The Hildebrand Rarity is not the most
exciting Bond adventure ever to make it into print but it works
quite nicely as a reverse murder mystery and certainly has a
memorable method of death for one character. This story is
not bad at all with an interesting character in Milton Krest -
who later turned up in the 1989 Bond film Licence To Kill.

For Your Eyes Only would be written by Richard Maibaum and
Michael G Wilson. Christopher Wood was now gone - as was

Lewis Gilbert. The fact that Wood and Gilbert would not be involved in For Your Eyes Only was an indication that Cubby Broccoli favoured a change of tone and direction. Tom Mankiewicz wrote a For Your Eyes Only treatment when it was supposed to be the next picture after The Spy Who Loved Me but this treatment was not an influence on the actual film we later got in 1981.

John Glen was announced as the director on For Your Eyes Only. This promotion was a reward for Glen's previous work on the Bond series. It has been reported that Glen was third choice to direct the new film and that Cubby even offered it to Peter Hunt at one point. If this story is true then Hunt obviously must have passed. John Glen directed all the eighties Bond films (For Your Eyes Only, Octopussy, A View to a Kill, The Living Daylights and Licence to Kill) and first began his long association with the series when he worked as an editor and second unit director on Peter Hunt's On Her Majesty's Secret Service in 1969. Before he directed the 80s Bonds, John Glen's finest hour was the pre-title sequence of The Spy Who Loved Me where Bond skis off a mountain range into infinity before his Union Jack parachute opens. It was Glen who hiked up a mountain in Baffin Island with his film unit to capture this legendary stunt.

After signing to direct For Your Eyes Only, John Glen's first task was to help find a new Bond actor because Roger Moore wasn't expected to come back. In 1980, EON brought the cultish New Zealander David Warbeck in for a three day screen test. Warbeck had been a Bond contender since the early 1970s. David Warbeck was 39 years-old now and at the start of his Italian horror and 'Macaroni Combat' phase. Warbeck would become something of a cult B-movie horror and action star in Italy. In the Billington v Warbeck battle of reserve Bonds it appears there was a very brief window in time here where Warbeck edged his nose in front. According to David Warbeck, he was selected to play Bond in the next film and John Hough (director of films such as The Legend of Hell House and Escape to Witch Mountain) was to direct.

"I can't recall what titles they were," said Hough. "What happened was that Roger Moore had entered into dispute with Cubby Broccoli over salary and this was something that was documented in Variety and the trade papers and Roger was looking for a hike in pay, and so, had decided that he wouldn't play Bond again unless he was paid an increase in salary. At this point the Bond company had decided they wouldn't do that and they would go with a new James Bond and a new director. They choose an actor called David Warbeck who was secretly tested. I had directed David Warbeck in a film called Wolfshead (aka Wolfshead: The Legend of Robin Hood), which is a very highly regarded little film.

"Cubby Broccoli had seen this and had decided that if David Warbeck got to play James Bond then I would get to direct Bonds. In fact, they did a two picture deal with me because they were going to do two James Bonds, back-to-back. The idea was, at that particular point, they wouldn't do just one James Bond at time but we were going to do two at a time. And so, two directors would both alternate and do a Bond each and the whole thing was pretty much set up. But before David Warbeck got the chance to sign the contract, Roger Moore had decided that he would go ahead and take the deal that was on the table. I knew that he and I would never work together because we had a dispute on the Saint TV series and we weren't compatible. The chance never arose past that point."

The Hough/Warbeck concept is sort of confusing in that Warbeck's test was directed by John Glen - who ended up directing the next film. Were Hough and Glen supposed to alternate on directing Bond films? David Warbeck said his proposed Bond film was nixed by a financial crash. This could be a reference to the failure of Heaven's Gate proving to be a box-office disaster for United Artists in 1980 though in his book (David Warbeck: the Man and His Movies), Warbeck said the Arab oil embargo caused studios to cut budgets, thus causing the back-to-back Bond idea to be dropped. Despite all of the auditions, in his memoir Cubby Broccoli said that United Artists were very pro-Roger Moore when it came to the

James Bond franchise in the early 80s. They felt that Roger was popular and established in the role and saw no need to make a change unless it was absolutely forced upon them.

Of his 1980 Bond audition, Warbeck said - "It's ironic that I was actually contracted to be the new Bond and my director was going to be Johnny Hough, because I had chats with Broccoli and said no, I didn't want to work with John Glen, because I have this problem with directors. John Glen and Martin Campbell, well the younger Martin Campbell were sort of similar in that they just didn't share my sense of humour and my sense of humour is based on experience and it's based on visual gags. For example, when I did the Bond bits with John Glen, there was a sequence where somebody sticks a gun in my back while I'm on the telephone and I thought it would be a great visual gag if when he says "put your hands up" you've still got the telephone in your hand with the cord attached. And so you whack him with the telephone and then you try to strangle him with the cord while the person on the other end is still talking! You see what I mean? It would have been a good visual as well as well as plot gag, but John Glen wouldn't see that."

David Warbeck said that his extensive screen test was at Pinewood with elaborate security. It was all very hush hush. The odd thing about Warbeck becoming the new Bond at that time is that his career was floundering somewhat and he still wasn't very well known - although of course Bond actors tend not to be tremendously famous when they are cast. EON have never cast an A'list star as Bond and probably never will. It actually tends to help if the new Bond actor isn't that well known because then it's easier for the audience to simply accept them as Bond. This is why, to give an example, many believe that Henry Cavill's Bond hopes became more remote when he was cast as Superman.

David Warbeck claimed that he was paid a salary by EON to be a substitute James Bond - ready to step in at a moment's notice should there be a problem with Roger Moore. It is obviously impossible to verify this but it doesn't seem impossible. Michael Billington was in a similar situation. David Warbeck's acting career was not exactly A'list but he was a wealthy man thanks to the many commercials and adverts he had done as a model. It would be fair to say that Warbeck was more enthusiastic about James Bond than Michael Billington. Billington would doubtless have been grateful for the money and career opportunities Bond would have afforded him but he wasn't actually much of a Bond fan in real life and yearned to do serious acting roles. Billington, like Timothy Dalton, was also quite reserved and private. Warbeck on the other hand would have absolutely loved becoming James Bond and completely embraced all the fame that came with it.

Despite the secret drama with David Warbeck, it was - no surprise here - Michael Billington who eventually came the closest to becoming the new James Bond in For Your Eyes Only. Billington was still very much in the loop and still close to the Broccoli family. When the start of shooting on For Your Eyes Only began to loom on the horizon, Michael Billington was flown to Corfu in case no deal with Roger could be negotiated. Billington was put in a tux (and later a black polo neck) and given a James Bondian photo shoot. 1980 was certainly an interesting year for Billington because he sold a screenplay which became the David Essex film Silver Dream Racer and moved to the United States to study acting with Lee Strasberg.

In 1980, the Daily News columnist Marilyn Beck wrote - 'Michael Billington has become the favoured date of Barbara Broccoli, the daughter of 007 producer Cubby Broccoli. And insiders are predicting Billington's sure to inherit the role of James Bond in For Your Eyes Only this fall - unless Roger and Cubby come to terms fast. Billington's name might not be familiar to you, but it certainly is to Moore. Because Broccoli has been conveniently keeping the unknown in the wings for years (cast him in a bit part in the 1977 The Spy Who Loved Me) and has frequently ribbed Roger that, if he got out of line, Michael would step into his 007 shoes. Moore thought Cubby was joking - until now.'

Michael Billington still looked good and would have made a credible and competent Bond circa 1980 had they needed a fresh last minute 007. Michael Billington was sterner and more serious than Roger - though not without a dry humour. Billington, one suspects, would sort of been like a vague cross between Timothy Dalton and Lewis Collins had he ever played James Bond. "Time passed and For Your Eyes Only was on the horizon," said Billington. "By this time the 'usual suspects' were gone. John Glen was at the helm; script by Richard Maibaum, close to retirement and Michael G Wilson, a lawyer by profession. The sharp and witty Christopher Woods dialogue was sadly no more. The troops were gathering to go to Corfu to begin filming but Roger was being coy. I think the money was an issue. Cubby had me fitted out with wardrobe and flew me to Corfu. We had a picture shoot."

Billington's enthusiasm for Bond, if his website (where he shared his memories of his acting career and brush with Bond fame) is anything to go by, seemed to be on the wane by this point. Billington said he didn't like For Your Eyes Only very much when he watched it. There was also a lot of speculation about Scottish actor David Robb - well known for playing Germanicus in the famous 1976 BBC production of I, Claudius - becoming the new Bond around this time. Years later Robb denied he'd ever had any contact regarding the role. Robb became well known to modern television viewers when he played played Dr Clarkson in Downton Abbey.

Other actors in the fray to replace Roger allegedly included Nicholas Clay, Michael Jayston, and Patrick Mower - though it's hard to believe any of these were serious candidates. It could be that Cubby Broccoli tested some of these actors as a tactic designed to put pressure on Roger to sign a contract. Mower was knocking on a bit by now and Michael Jayston was no spring chicken either. Nicholas Clay, one of the stars of John Boorman's Excalibur, had youth on his side and was very handsome but he wasn't the greatest actor in the world.

Martin Shaw, one of the stars of the daft but cultish police action show The Professionals along with Lewis Collins, said he was invited to do a James Bond screen test after Moonraker by Barbara Broccoli but declined this invitation - much to the surprise of Barbara. Martin Shaw said that playing Bond would overshadow anything else he ever did as an actor and he didn't want this to happen. Another actor who had flown onto the Broccoli family radar in relation to Bond was the fairly well known American star James Brolin. Brolin would be a very serious candidate for 007 a few years later.

EON were clearly preparing themselves for the imminent departure of Roger and looking high and low for a potential replacement. Maud Adams was secretly brought in to play audition scenes with the prospective Bond actors. At this precise moment in time the odds were mostly in favour of Michael Billington steeping into 007's polished shoes but - as ever - a last minute deal was put in place for Roger to return. In truth, Cubby, John Glen, and United Artists all wanted Roger to return and Roger wanted to come back to. It was just a question of his fee. John Glen in particular was desperate for Roger to come back because he just wanted to make a Bond film and didn't want the hassle of having to bed in a new Bond actor.

"To be honest I did want to make another film," said Roger Moore of this highly uncertain period. "This was all part of the bargaining ploy on EON's side - let it be known they were testing others so I'd take the deal on the table for fear of losing the part. Fair enough, we all enjoy a game of poker. I'm quite principled about not undervaluing my worth. If someone wants me for a job then I believe they should pay me a fair fee. My agent usually haggles it up a bit, the producer usually haggles it down a bit and a happy middle ground is found. If someone undervalues me, I simply walk away. I have no qualms about it."

When they began pre-production on For Your Eyes Only it was deemed very unlikely that Roger Moore would be back so they hired a number of stuntmen with black hair because the prime candidates to become the new 007 were dark haired actors like James Brolin and Michael Billington. When they learned that Roger was coming back they had to hurriedly get all their fair haired stuntmen back! With Roger back in place, the rest of the film now had to be cast.

The French actress Carole Bouquet was cast as Melina Havelock - the female lead. Cubby Broccoli and John Glen were in agreement on Bouquet and signed her up fairly quickly.

Bouquet was still in her early twenties and around thirty years younger than Roger Moore. The Italian actress Ornella Muti, forever immortal for her role as Princess Aura in the campy classic Flash Gordon, would later claim that she turned down the part of Melina Havelock before it went to Carole Bouquet. Ornella Muti even claimed that the role of Melina was specially written for her. I suspect there is an alternative Bond universe where For Your Eyes Only had Flash Gordon co-stars Timothy Dalton and Ornella Muti as the leads! That could feasibly have happened if Roger hadn't come back and EON were more persuasive.

Topol, another Flash Gordon star, was cast as Milos Columbo on the suggestion of Cubby Broccoli's wife Dana. Julian Glover, who plays Aristotle Kristatos, was no stranger to EON because he had auditioned to play Bond in Live and Let Die. Glover had appeared in everything from Quatermass and the Pit to the Empire Strikes Back to Doctor who. Lynn-Holly Johnson, who plays Bibi Dahl in for Your Eyes Only, used to be a professional ice skater. Johnson won the silver medal at the novice level of the 1974 U.S. Figure Skating Championships.

Michael Gothard was cast as the mysterious villain Emile Leopold Locque in the film. Gothard was an interesting actor in that he was a familiar face and had done lots of stuff but without ever threatening to become famous. Gothard was quite sinister looking so never got leading man roles - which may have frustrated him. He was a very interesting actor though. He had appeared in films like The Three Musketeers, Warlords of Atlantis, and Scream and Scream Again. His television roles included The Professionals, Randall and Hopkirk, and Shoestring.

M actor Bernard Lee sadly passed away from cancer early in the production on For Your Eyes Only. As a mark of respect, Cubby Broccoli did not recast the part for the movie. This is why Bond is briefed by James Villiers as Bill Tanner in For Your Eyes Only. Villiers expected to be the new regular M in the Bond franchise but was dispensed with after this movie as Cubby Broccoli thought he looked too young to be briefing Roger Moore. Villiers was said to be annoyed at being let go. Cubby Broccoli said that Bernard Lee's death cast a sad aura over the production. Lee had tried to come in and do a scene but he was too weak to complete it.

One of the cast members of For Your Eyes Only was the Australian actress Cassandra Harris as Countess Lisl von Schlaf. Harris had recently got married to a young Irish actor named Pierce Brosnan. At the time, Brosnan's credits only amounted to small roles in The Long Good Friday and The Mirror Crack'd. During the production of the film, Cassandra Harris introduced Brosnan to Cubby Broccoli and Broccoli immediately made a mental note of Brosnan as a potential future Bond. Brosnan was dark haired, tall, very handsome, and very charming. Cubby thought that if Brosnan could polish up his acting skills he'd make a perfect James Bond in the not too distant future.

The producers considered bringing Jaws back in For Your Eyes Only but decided in the end that he would clash with the more down to earth (for the Roger Moore era at least) tone of the film. Victor Tourjansky makes his third and last comedy cameo in For Your Eyes Only as the surprised 'man with glass of wine' on the slopes. Charles Dance had his first film role in For Your Eyes Only as Claus.

John Barry did not score For Your Eyes Only due to tax reasons (again). That task went to Bill Conti. It's probably fair to say that Conti's score is one of the most dated in the entire franchise! 80`s punk band Blondie recorded a For Your Eyes Only theme song. However, when Blondie were asked to record the song again to improve it they declined to do so and Sheena Easton was hired instead - even featuring in the title sequence. Maurice Binder thought that Sheena Easton was a beautiful woman so why not just have perform the song in the credits? Sheena Easton shot her contribution to the title sequence of For Your Eyes Only in just a single day. Easton later become most famous for her music association with Prince.

The helicopter PTS in For Your Eyes Only was suggested by the director John Glen. Cubby Broccoli didn't care much for the idea because he didn't think it was exciting enough to open a Bond film. However, they couldn't think of anything else so Cubby eventually gave the go ahead to Glen to shoot the helicopter sequence. Use of miniature model helicopters was combined with real helicopter footage in the sequence. The helicopter PTS in For Your Eyes Only was shot at the abandoned Beckton Gas Works in London. This was where Stanley Kubrick later shot parts of Full Metal Jacket.

In the PTS of For Your Eyes Only, most people are baffled when the ersatz Blofeld (impaled on Bond's helicopter) says - "I'll buy you delicatessen in stainless steel!" This line was suggested by Cubby Broccoli. Apparently it was an old saying that New York mafia people would say when they wanted to negotiate or do business. The writers on the film hated the delicatessen line but Cubby was the boss so it ended up in the movie.

In the pre-title sequence a helicopter is sent for Bond but, flying over Westminster, the helicopter is placed on remote control by a man in a wheelchair who looks an awful lot like Blofeld (although not identified as such). EON's ability to use Blofeld had been compromised by the tangled legal web spun by Kevin McClory. It's a nose thumb at Kevin McClory. Up yours Mr McClory. We're going to drop thinly veiled fake Blofeld down a chimney.

The ski scene in For Your Eyes Only was shot in Cortina d'Ampezzo, Italy, in the Alps. The producers had a big problem though because there was hardly any snow there at the time. They had to import ice, snow, and powder to lend an appropriately ice-glazed backdrop. Roger Moore actually became a very accomplished skier after moving to Switzerland in the 1970s. Even so, he wasn't allowed to ski in the James Bond films for insurance and safety reasons. The keel-hauling sequence from Fleming's Live and Let Die novel was supposed to take place in the 1973 movie of the same name. In the end it appeared in For Your Eyes Only.

Bond driving a humble Citroën 2CV for a chase in For Your Eyes Only is a very pointed reaction to the fact that critics had complained about the Bond films becoming too gadget festooned and outlandish. At one point during the shooting of For Your Eyes Only, they actually slipped an outtake of Carole Bouquet into a scene because they were finding it so difficult to get her to smile! The outtake moment was of Bouquet laughing at a cheeky joke by Roger Moore. Roger Moore said he got banged up quite badly shooting the ice hockey sequence in For Your Eyes Only. Roger said in his memoir that although people tend to think of For Your Eyes Only as more grounded and serious than his other films he didn't notice any departure in tone or style at all when he was actually making the film!

After the excesses of Moonraker it was decided to make For Your Eyes Only more of a spy thriller and tone down the gadgets and special effects. For Your Eyes Only tends to be generally well regarded by fans as a consequence. This film eschews the space-age gadgetry of the previous two Roger Moore entries. The plot of the film revolves around the sinking of the spy ship St Georges, which was equipped with an ATAC missile communication device.

James Bond is sent on the trail of this device and teams up with Melina Havelock (Carole Bouquet), out for revenge after witnessing the murder of her Marine archaeologist father Sir Timothy Havelock on his yacht. Sir Timothy, a Secret Service operative, was also after the ATAC before his death and Bond soon has his hands full restraining the crossbow wielding Melina from her revenge mission and trying to work out if Columbo (Topol) or Kristatos (Julian Glover) is the real enemy.

For Your Eyes Only saw the promotion of second-unit director and editor John Glen to full-fledged director and the underrated Glen makes his presence felt with some excellent action sequences. The pre-credit sequence is a bit daft but good fun and begins with Bond placing some flowers on the grave of his late wife Teresa "Tracy" Bond. It's a nice moment and was originally conceived for a new James Bond actor. This scene was intended to be a continuity moment for a new 007. When Moore had a last minute change of heart (as he usually did!) it was left in the film and actually works very well, giving Moore's Bond a resigned, slightly weary moment of reflection.

A helicopter is then sent for Bond but, flying over Westminster, the helicopter is placed on remote control by a man in a wheelchair who looks an awful lot like Blofeld (although not identified as such). EON's ability to use Blofeld had been compromised by Kevin McClory so this PTS is a bit on the cheeky side. Bond has to regain control of the helicopter by clambering outside it in a very entertaining sequence that features some excellent model work by the great Derek Meddings.

Maurice Binder's usual nicely done title sequence is quite unusual here in that it features Sheena Easton onscreen within the titles singing the theme song, which is pleasant enough as Bond songs go. The film opens with the sinking of the St Georges, which has been disguised as a fishing trawler. It's a very effective sequence with good work again by Derek Meddings. There are some good set-pieces in For Your Eyes

Only on the whole including a ski-chase that involves
motorbikes and a bobsleigh run, an assault on an Albanian
dockside and a mountain climbing sequence which leads to the
climax on a remote monastery.

My one gripe with these action sequences is that some of them
perhaps go on for too long - which is a common complaint in
Roger's films. For Your Eyes Only is definitely a film that could
have lost ten or fifteen minutes. The mountain climbing
sequence, for example, while well-staged, and intentionally
back to basics after the outrageous mayhem of Roger's
previous two Bond films, does go on a bit. We know Bond isn't
going to fall off and die so there is only so much tension to be
generated!

I suspect that the climbing sequence was probably written
when they presumed they were going to have a new - and
obviously - younger actor. Roger seems a bit on the old side to
be climbing mountains! There is also an underwater
submersible scene that slows the film down in my opinion and
drags somewhat. It is hard not to stifle a yawn when that
yellow submersible craft is onscreen for what seems like way
too much time. With the possible exception of the ski-chase,
perhaps the best action sequence in For Your Eyes Only
involves Bond and Melina in a country car chase ("I love a
drive in the country. Don't you...?") in a battered Citroën 2CV.
We do also get to see Roger Moore driving a Lotus again
which, let's be honest, is always fun.

The casting in For Your Eyes Only is reasonably good on the
whole. Julian Glover is fine as Kristatos and displays different
facets to his character in order to achieve his ends. Carole
Bouquet is one of the most striking Bond girls but not the
greatest actress in the world. Her chemistry with Roger Moore
in the film is almost like a father and daughter team with the
disparity in their ages but they do work nicely together at
times. Roger has an excellent snowy scene on a horse-drawn
sledge where he tries to persuade Melina to calm down and be
more rational.

The pair are also good in the keel-hauling sequence, taken from the Live And Let Die novel. It's one of the highlights of For Your Eyes Only with Bond and Melina battling coral and sharks as they are dragged along underwater. Elsewhere, Topol is decent enough as Columbo and brings his customary enthusiasm to the film. Lynn-Holly Johnson as Bibi Dahl, a young skater financed by the villain of the film, is perhaps though one addition too many to the cast. It was probably a wise move to have Roger's Bond rebuff her advances and offer to buy her an ice-cream instead!

Series regulars Desmond Llewelyn, Lois Maxwell and Walter Gotell are back again and Q has a funny scene where he poses as a priest in a Confessional Booth to meet Bond. John Wyman as Erich Kriegler makes a decent and very physical henchman and Michael Gothard is suitably creepy as Emile Leopold Loque. Roger is fine in the film and has his most cold-blooded moment as 007 when he kicks a car over a cliff. For Your Eyes Only gives him his usual quota of one-liners and chases but he does get some quieter, more introspective/restrained moments in the film for a change and plays them very well. Roger's 007 is more cold blooded here at times and less jokey than usual but Rog could play a straight scene with more competence than anyone gave him credit for. He's often very good in the film.

For Your Eyes Only is though the first film where Roger Moore's age is starting to become, well, noticeable. He looks a bit thick in the waist in this film and Roger suddenly seems like he's a hundred years old when playing scenes with young Lynn-Holly Johnson as Bibi Dahl. You can understand why some Bond fans think For Your Eyes Only would have been the best place for Roger to bow out gracefully. Roger still often looks very handsome in the film though. It's just simply the case that he seems to have aged somewhat since Moonraker.

The end of the film has Janet Brown and John Wells in comic cameos as (Prime Minister) Margaret Thatcher and her husband Dennis. This comedy scene seems rather out of place

in the movie and should have been left on the cutting room
floor. Apart from some the action sequences going on for too
long and some draggy moments, the biggest problem the film
has is Bill Conti's eccentric disco score - which was probably
dated about a week after its completion. Some of the action
cues are very good but overall it's an eccentric and somewhat
jarring score. It's a great shame that John Barry skipped this
one.

For Your Eyes Only is not perfect but it has some lovely
Mediterranean backdrops and is a likeable attempt to bring
the Roger Moore era back to Earth. I find the film a trifle
overrated myself because For Your Eyes Only has some dull
spots for me and I don't care for the music score too much. For
Your Eyes Only doesn't have the fun factor of Roger's other
Bond pictures for me personally but I would concede that it is
a very decent and laudable attempt to go back to a few basics
after the outlandish mayhem and comedy shenanigans of
Moonraker.

CHAPTER EIGHT - OCTOPUSSY

For Your Eyes Only was premiered at the Odeon Leicester Square in London on 24 June 1981. Prince Charles and the then Lady Diana Spencer were in attendance. This was one of Diana's early royal engagements so she was the centre of attention. Princess Margaret also attended the event. Cassandra Harris attended with her husband Pierce Brosnan - who was sporting a dapper mustache. Harry Saltzman was also a guest at the premiere. It was a nice touch by Cubby Broccoli to invite him. It was apparently Topol who suggested to Cubby he should invite Harry. The marketing campaign for the movie, as one might expect, was highly professional with toys, a brochure, a Marvel comic adaptation, toy guns, 007 watches, a children's annual, and more besides.

There was a bit of a rumpus over the poster for the movie - which depicted Bond shooting through the legs of a girl wearing next to nothing. The poster was cropped, censored, and banned in some places in the United States for being too risque. The media attempted to find out who the model in the poster was and eventually deduced it was Joyce Bartle - a 22 year-old model from New York. "I was embarrassed that I had to prove that the legs were mine," said Bartle. "You know your own legs when you see them!"

Though many Bond fans today tend to think of For Your Eyes Only as one of the best of Roger's Bond movies it met with fairly unenthusiastic reviews at time. 'For Your Eyes Only', wrote a grudging New York Times, 'is not the best of the series by a long shot - that would be a choice between Goldfinger and Moonraker - but it's far from the worst. It has a structural problem in that it opens with a precredit helicopter chase - in, over, around and through London - which is so lunatic and inventive that the rest of the movie is hard-put to achieve such a fever-pitch again.'

Gary Arnold in The Washington Post called the film 'ponderous' and said it never really seemed to spark into life.

Derek Malcom in The Guardian also said he thought the film was boring. Jay Scott of The Globe and Mail called For Your Eyes Only one of the worst films of 1981 - which was utterly preposterous if you ask me. There are hundreds of films in 1981 worse than For Your Eyes Only.

TIME magazine was in an especially snotty mood and didn't care for the film much. 'At the end one must remind oneself that human beings—actors, actually—are also involved in the enterprise. Carole Bouquet (23, long dark hair, Aegean-blue eyes, lissome frame) is the love interest, and more: a warrior goddess who saves Bond's life at least as often as he saves hers, and a welcome addition to this summer's gallery of can-do heroines. Topol, as the wily Greek smuggler Columbo, should be in the "Guinness Book of Word Wreckers"; he is perhaps the first performer to demonstrate the art of overacting by chewing pistachio nuts. Then there is Roger Moore, haberdasher's delight and director's despair. Moore's mannequin good looks and waxed-fruit insouciance have brought him far in movies; this is his fifth Bond picture. But beneath his suave double-entendres and amplified body blows, one can hear the sound of expensive gears meshing—for Moore is merely the best-oiled cog in this perpetual motion machine.'

There were though some positive reviews. Variety wrote - 'For Your Eyes Only bears not the slightest resemblance to the Ian Fleming novel of the same title, but emerges as one of the most thoroughly enjoyable of the 12 Bond pix [to date] despite fact that many of the usual ingredients in the successful 007 formula are missing. The film is probably the best-directed on all levels since On Her Majesty's Secret Service, as John Glen, moving into the director's chair after long service as second unit director and editor, displays a fine eye. Story also benefits from presence of a truly sympathetic heroine, fetchingly portrayed by Carole Bouquet, who exhibits a humanity and emotionalism not frequently found in this sort of pop adventure and who takes a long time (the entire picture, in fact) to jump into the sack with him. M is gone, due to Bernard

Lee's death; Bond doesn't make his first feminine conquest until halfway through the picture; there's no technology introduced by Q which saves the hero in the end; no looming supervillain dominates the drama; Bond bon mots are surprisingly sparse, and the fate of the whole world isn't even hanging in the balance at the climax.'

Though the reviews were mixed, many critics did at least seem to appreciate the fact that For Your Eyes Only had dialled back on the gadgetry and technology for a change. It was noticeable though that For Your Eyes Only was the first Bond movie where the critics were starting to mention the fact that Roger Moore was starting to look a bit on the mature side to be romancing young supermodel type women and climbing mountains. Roger would be 55 by the time the next film came out so you can understand why there was a lot of doubt that he'd be back.

During the press junket for the movie, Cubby Broccoli and Roger Moore were evasive when it came to the question of whether or not Roger would play Bond again. Cubby had already announced that Octopussy would be the next Bond movie. The Bond series would go on but would it be with Roger or someone else? For Your Eyes Only was a solid enough hit, earning $195.3 million from a $28 million budget. This was down on Moonraker but the Bond franchise was still in good health and still making plans for the future. For Your Eyes Only was the last Bond film to be released by United Artists before their merger/buy out with MGM.

In 1981 a new series of James Bond books began and it was John Gardner who had the enviable/unenviable task of writing them and trying to fill the late Ian Fleming's shoes. Gardner was not Vladimir Nabokov (or even Kingsley Amis for that matter, Amis once the author of an excellent Bond novel called Colonel Sun) but was seen as a solid sort who could churn out a thriller fairly rapidly. His James Bond continuation novels tended to divide opinion on the whole with some enjoying the cinematic nature of the plots and feeling they were actually better than the scripts EON were conjuring up for the films. However, EON never used any of Gardner's books for the films and Gardner seemed irritated by this in some interviews.

Cubby hired George MacDonald Fraser to work on the screenplay for Octopussy. George MacDonald Fraser drafted the first screenplay for Octopussy and then the story was polished by Richard Maibaum and Michael G Wilson. Fraser, author of the Flashman books, came up with the idea of setting the film in India. Octopussy and The Living Daylights is the fourteenth and final James Bond book by Ian Fleming and was published posthumously in 1966. There are four stories in this slim volume - two of which were added in later additions. The first story is called Octopussy. A murder victim called Hans Oberhauser is found frozen in an Austrian glacier and James Bond is sent to Jamaica to talk to the last man to see the victim before his death. This just happens to be a certain Major Dexter Smythe. Bond is personally involved in the case as Oberhauser was a mentor to him in his younger days after the death of his parents.

The second story is called The Property of a Lady. A communications clerk with British Intelligence called Maria Freudenstein is a double agent working for the Soviets. M has been on to Freudenstein for ages though and feeds her false information but he is curious to see what her reward from the Russians will be as she doesn't seem to have much in the bank beyond her clerk's salary. When Freudenstein suspiciously 'inherits' a Fabergé egg to auction at Sotheby's, Bond points out that a major KGB figure will have to be secretly present to bid for it and therefore push the price up to cover her services to them. Bond duly attends the auction to look for the KGB representative.

The third story is called The Living Daylights. A British agent known as '272' is heading back to the West through Berlin and the Soviets are sending their top assassin - codenamed 'Trigger' - to shoot him as he makes his way across no-man's land. M sends James Bond to kill the KGB assassin and 007 hunkers down in a safe house with his sniper rifle waiting for a shot at his target, watching what appears to be a female orchestra go in and out of the building he is keeping watch on. The Living Daylights is an interesting story and the strongest one here. It revolves around Bond's distaste for killing - despite it often being his job. This story was incorporated into the beginning of the 1987 Timothy Dalton film of the same name in (for the film series) faithful fashion and presents us with a more weary, tired Bond who is questioning his profession and the things he has to do in the name of Queen and Country.

The final short story is called 007 in New York and is by far the shortest of the four on offer. The story first appeared in US editions of Fleming's non-fiction book Thrilling Cities which collected some travel pieces he had written for the Sunday Times. In this story James Bond is sent to New York to tell a former MI6 secretary that the man she lives with is a KGB agent. This secret trip by 007 is a courtesy afforded to her by M for loyal service in the past. Bond arranges to meet her at Central Park Zoo and thinks about a woman called Solange who he will also see later. 007 in New York is a mildly interesting trifle that consists of Bond's general musings about New York and also a lot about food and where he will go to eat. Martinis at the Plaza and dinner at Grand Central's Oyster Bar etc. Of the four stories in the collection, it is only The Property of a Lady which features in the movie Octopussy.

Once again the familiar game of poker over Roger's fee led to more Bond auditions and interviews. These interviews included a very obvious candidate - Lewis Collins. To people in Britain at least, Lewis Collins was the James Bond that got away. It's impossible to watch The Professionals or the 1982 action film Who Dares Wins and not think that Collins would have made a terrific Bond. Collins is believed to have had a meeting with Cubby Broccoli circa 1982. He was in his mid thirties at the time. Collins was tough, sardonic, and good at action and fights. He was a little on the short side but he had black hair and a good look for Bond. Lewis Collins would have brought the franchise back to earth and played a tougher sort of Bond but he was good with humour too and always seemed to layer a self-deprecation into his characters.

"I think it is time for a change, although no one has approached me," said Lewis Collins of James Bond in the early eighties. "What I would be interested in is a new character, starting from scratch - an Eighties version of Bond, getting away from the gadgets a bit. When Connery started you really believed he could kill someone with his bare hands. He was an animal, but a smooth one. Since then, Bond has been watered down. I think what the Bond films need is a more gripping storyline. The public needs to be more involved with the character. You need a human being the public cares about."

Lewis Collins had signed a three film contract with producer Euan Lloyd which was projected to make him a big star. "He's a strong actor with a lot of charisma and I'm sure that with a major campaign behind him he will become a big star," said Lloyd. Things didn't quite go according to plan though. Who Dares Wins (in which Collins plays an SAS captain who foils an embassy siege) was completed but the second proposed film, Wild Geese 2, saw Collins replaced by Scott Glenn. The third film in the Collins/Lloyd contract was supposed to be an action film about the Falklands War but this film never got made. As a consequence of all of this Lewis Collins never became a movie star.

The person who came closest to being cast as Roger's replacement this time around was not Lewis Collins though, nor even EON's beloved Michael Billington, but the American actor James Brolin. Brolin was 43 and had appeared in films like The Amityville Horror and Westworld. In 1981, Brolin had shown his action man credentials in the adventure film high Risk. He was 6'3, handsome, and suave. Brolin did an extensive screen test with Octopussy stars Maud Adams and Vijay Amritraj and at one point was very close to signing on the dotted line. You could say that Brolin was sort of like the 1980s version of John Gavin when it came to Bond. Close but no cigar.

Brolin did his audition in an American accent because they simply wanted to get a feel for how Brolin looked and how he would play a Bondian sort of scene. He would obviously have had to have worked on an English accent later. Brolin looks terrific in his screen test although he is a trifle wooden. Whether he would have made a good Bond is open to question but there's no doubt he would have looked good in a tux. John Glen, who directed Brolin's Bond auditions, said that testing Brolin was merely a tactic designed to put pressure on Roger Moore to accept terms for Octopussy. Brolin claimed though that he was making preparations to move to London and shoot Octopussy when he learned that Roger was coming back.

Cubby Broccoli even toyed with the idea of offering Superman star Christopher Reeve the part of James Bond in an effort to jolt Roger into signing a contract. Oliver Tobias also auditioned to play Bond in Octopussy. The Swiss born actor was about 35 at the time. His film roles included Arabian Adventure and The Stud. The Stud made Tobias something of a sex symbol at the time. He never really became a film star but he did have a solid career with plenty of good television work. Tobias, like Brolin, did a fight scene at Pinewood as part of his test.

Still in contention was Michael Billington. This would be the last time though that Billington was a Bond candidate. He was now 41 years-old. Billington had moved to the United States at this time to enhance his acting career but he didn't have much luck. Billington was cast as Count Louis Dardinay in an action adventure show called The Quest produced by Stephen J. Cannell but The Quest was cancelled after five episodes in 1982. Gratuitous Bond related trivia - Billington only got the part of Count Louis Dardinay because Louis Jourdan turned it down. If you look on YouTube you can watch the pilot episode for The Quest and it's clear that Billington was still more than capable of playing Bond. He is crisp and commanding and still looks the part. A couple of years later Billington appeared in

the television movie Antony and Cleopatra. One of his co-stars
was a certain Timothy Dalton.

'Octopussy rolled around,' wrote Billington on his website
years later. 'I tested with with Deborah Sheldon and Susan
Penhaligon but it was purely cosmetic. I didn't feel John Glenn
was truly an actors director'. And anyway he seemed more
secure with Roger so, in my view; he needed me and any other
candidate for that matter, like acute pneumonia. And with all
respect, Michael G Wilson was not really a writer. And with all
the will in the world, I couldn't quite see myself dressed as a
circus clown clutching a Faberge Egg, and the finale with the
ticking time bomb was in my view a resurrected dead turkey,
so consequently I was uncharacteristically very, very nervous
of the prospects.' Octopussy would be the last time that
Michael Billington had a plausible shot at becoming James
Bond.

In the end, Roger Moore returned to make Octopussy. One of
the main reasons why they wanted Roger back was the
planned release of the unofficial Bond film Never Say Never
Again with Sean Connery in 1983. EON wanted an established
Bond rather than a new actor to go up against Connery. In the
end they needn't have worried. An agreement was reached for
the films to be released at different times. Some film rushes
(basically footage that hasn't been edited) from Never Say
Never Again were sent to the Octopussy production offices by
mistake at one point. EON were perfect gentlemen about this.
They arranged for the rushes to be sent back and made sure no
one viewed them.

Despite all the Battle of the Bonds headlines, Roger Moore and
Sean Connery remained friends and even had dinner a few
times while these films were in production. Curiously, it was
later revealed that Kevin McClory had planned two remakes of
Thunderball at this time and wanted Magnum star Tom
Selleck to play Bond in the second film. This obviously didn't
happen in the end. It was a bit of a pipedream to imagine he
could make two versions of Thunderball - let alone persuade

Tom Selleck to play James Bond.

An impressive and colourful cast was assembled for Never Say Never Again around Connery. Klaus Maria Brandauer would play Largo while Max von Sydow would be Blofeld. Edward Fox and Alec McCowen would be M and Q respectively while Barbara Carrera and Kim Basinger would become the latest (unofficial) Bond girls - one good one bad in the classic tradition. It appeared that the ingredients for a classic film, or at least a very good one, might be in place but Never Say Never Again would be hamstrung by budget problems (a lack of spectacle and action is a frequent criticism of the film) and many production troubles.

Louis Jourdan, who had turned down the part of Drax in Moonraker, agreed to take the role of the villain Kamal Khan in Octopussy. The Indian actor Kabir Bedi was cast as his henchman Gobinda. Steven Berkoff was cast as the 'secondary' villain General Orlov. Vijay Amritraj, who played Vijay in Octopussy, was a professional tennis player (which would explain the tennis sight gags in Octopussy). Amritraj was a friend of Cubby Broccoli and simply asked Cubby if he could be in a Bond film. Robert Brown proves a good solid appointment as M. Is Brown supposed to be his character from The Spy Who Loved Me? A promoted Admiral Hargreaves? This is arguably the best theory to accept.

Maud Adams made history when she took the title role in Octopussy as she had already played a Bond Girl in The Man with the Golden Gun. Adams had been brought in to act in the auditions with potential Bond actors so they eventually figured they might as well just put her in the film! Persis Khambatta, of Star Trek: The Motion Picture fame, was considered as the title character but lost out to Maud Adams. Susie Coelho was also considered for the title role in Octopussy. Coelho is an English born actress and businesswoman of Indian heritage. Barbara Carrera claims she turned down the title role in Octopussy so she could appear in Never Say Never Again. There was a lot of press speculation that B'movie star Sybil

Danning was going to be the female lead in Octopussy but this turned out to be hot air and had no basis in fact.

Kristina Wayborn as Magda broke some toes shooting a scene in Octopussy when her character has to kick a weapon out of a goon's hand. The bazooka she had to kick was supposed to be plastic but turned out to be metal. Bond ordering the tiger to "sit!" in Octopussy is a reference to Barbara Woodhouse. Barbara Woodhouse was a dog trainer who often appeared on British television in the 1980s. The elephant hunt in Octopussy was originally supposed to take place in The Man with the Golden Gun. The PTS of Octopussy, though set in Cuba, was actually shot at RAF Northolt in London. They simply added a few fake palm trees.

Stuntman Martin Grace suffered terrible injuries on the set of Octopussy when shooting at the Nene Valley Railway in Peterborough with a solid wall hitting him as he clung to the train, smashing his pelvis and thigh bones. As Roger Moore marvelled when recalling the incident, it was Grace's incredible tenacity, strength and courage that helped him to not only survive but return to action for the next Bond adventure. Production on Octopussy was briefly halted when Roger Moore appeared to have heart problems. It turned out to be a false alarm though and he was given a clean bill of health.

The greatest of all the Bond inspired heroes came to the screen in 1981's Raiders Of The Lost Ark. Adventurer/archaeologist Indiana Jones came off as an all-American mixture of James Bond and Allan Quatermain in a glorious update of the cliffhanger Republic serials and Gunga Din. Lucas and Spielberg have both acknowledged 007 as part of the inspiration for Raiders. Octopussy's big plane sequence and some of the jungle capers feel like they were inspired by Raiders.

John Barry was back for Octopussy and the main song for the film was the ballad All Time High sung by Rita Coolidge and written by Tim Rice. John Barry made sure that he used the Bond theme a lot in Octopussy because it obviously couldn't feature in Never Say Never Again. This was the main handicap facing Never Say Never Again. It wouldn't be able to have all the Bond tropes like the gunbarrell, the Binder titles, and the Bond music.

What Octopussy lacks in coherence it makes up for with fun and nonsense. This is not the most serious of Bond films but the dollars are there on the screen and the return of John Barry is like a magical masking tape that makes you more forgiving than you should be. With John Barry's arrangements it just feels much more like James Bond. The plot of Octopussy contains priceless Faberge eggs, jewel smuggling, female circus performers in colourful lycra, and a nutty Russian General (Steven Berkhoff) with dastardly plans for a strike against the West.

This cheeky smuggling racket has the potential to threaten the safety of Western Europe as James Bond takes on sarcastic and very smooth Afghan prince Kamal Khan (Louis Jordan) and the completely mad General Orlov. Throw in Maud Adams as the enigmatic Octopussy and locations that include India and Germany and you have a highly enjoyable two hours or so. After the less exuberant but interesting For Your Eyes Only, Octopussy returned the series to widescreen spectacle. The plot has more holes than a garden invaded by moles in a gigantic mechanical digger but Octopussy is a very lavish production intent on entertaining the audience.

Take the PTS as an example, one of the most outrageous in the series. Bond takes control of a miniature Acrostar jet in an unnamed Central American country and dodges a heat-seeking missile before destroying an aircraft hanger in spectacular fashion. Maurice Binder's (yes, you guessed it) octopus themed titles and the naff but strangely enjoyable ditty 'All Time High', sung by Rita Coolidge, are both very acceptable.

For all its charming nonsense, there is an atmospheric enough start to Octopussy when a pursued 009 tries to bring a fake Faberge egg across the Berlin wall to alert the authorities about a possible funding source for Russian agents. Roger is soon supplied with an amusing scene where he bids against Kamal khan at Sotheby's in an experimental ruse and the film speedily moves to India where the customary chases and jokes ensue. Bond and the urbane Khan are soon crossing wits over a game of backgammon. "Double sixes. Fancy that!"

There is a lot of action in Octopussy. The chases through the streets of India sometimes become too comic (tennis sight gags, as we noted, are included as a nod to the presence of Vijay Amritraj in the cast as a contact of 007) but the Yo-Yo razor saws look very nasty, throwing an element of danger into the film. I do like the moment where Bond pushes a heavy into a giant fish tank. The romantic depiction of India in the film is very James Bond franchise. The Indian locations veer towards travelogue and the comedy sight gags during some of the many chases there are sometimes wearisome but Octopussy is generally good undemanding fun and what's wrong with that?

Steven Berkoff hams it up as General Orlov and has a lot of fun. In a more serious film he might have stood out a lot more! Walter Gotell has a slightly expanded role as General Gogol, here the dove to Orlov's hawk, while the dependable Robert Brown takes over as M after the sad death of the great Bernard Lee. Lois Maxwell and Desmond Llewelyn are naturally on hand for some banter and gadgets respectively as Moneypenny and Q. "Double-o seven on an island populated exclusively by women? We won't see him till dawn!"

David Meyer and Anthony Meyer are also a clever addition as twin henchmen from Octopussy's circus. Both are expert knife chuckers. There's a good circus train sequence in Octopussy that goes on a fair bit but does feature some very dangerous stuntwork. Regarding the cast, I also enjoy Kabir Bedi's amusingly stonefaced henchman Gobinda.

Roger, who was nearly replaced prior to shooting, brings his usual suave sense of mischief to Octopussy. The film gives him some nice comic moments and jokes, if perhaps one or two too many. He's on his last legs as far as his 007 tenure goes but Octopussy serves as a final epic Bond. I actually think Roger is very good in the infamous and much maligned sequence where he has to defuse the nuclear bomb dressed as a clown. A bit of tension is extracted and you are reminded of the actor staggering out of that centrifuge in Moonraker. Roger Moore had an uncanny knack of keeping his head above water in very big, outrageous films, a quality that was sometimes overlooked.

It should be noted though that Roger in Octopussy is clearly getting too old for this **** - as Danny Glover might say. It is becoming rather implausible for us to believe that Roger's Bond is capable of doing all these death defying stunts and seducing beautiful young women! You could argue that Octopussy was one film too many for Rog but he was so established in the part by now that you can understand why EON kept him on. If you were a very young person or kid in 1983 then Sean Connery in Never Say Never again was the interloper while Roger was the incumbent!

Octopussy is typical of the lavish production and grand-scale mayhem that Cubby Broccoli brought to the James Bond series. Regardless of the tone/direction of any specific film, this widescreen sense of scope is something much missed from the franchise these days. For some reason Bond films just don't fill the screen the way they used to. Octopussy may be frowned on by purists but the film is always pleasurable enough for those who enjoy the Roger Moore era.

CHAPTER NINE - A VIEW TO A KILL

Octopussy benefited from a spirited marketing campaign which also dovetailed into the fact that the Bond franchise was celebrating its 21st anniversary. There were two documentaries and the usual battery of 'merch' and commercial brand deals. There were toys, watches, badges, key-rings, stickers, brochures, and all manner of Bond and Octopussy related stuff for collectors and 007 fans. In Britain, Smiths Crisps promoted the movie while Nabisco breakfast cereals did a similar thing in the United States. Octopussy premiered at the Odeon Leicester Square on 6 June 1983, with Prince Charles and Diana, Princess of Wales, in attendance to meet the cast and crew. Celebrities at the premiere included Tom Selleck, Liza Minelli, and the tennis champion John McEnroe.

There was supposed to be an Octopussy video game by the Parker Brothers. The game would have featured a train section and other elements from the movie. It was widely promoted in magazines and would have been the first video game tie-in for a Bond film. However the game was behind schedule and not very good so it was scrapped. The company then hired a new team to complete a new game called James Bond 007. This new game was a very uninspired Moon Patrol clone and mashes up elements from Diamonds Are Forever, The Spy Who Loved Me, Moonraker, and For Your Eyes Only. It was released on the Atari systems and later the Commodore 64. The game got poor reviews and has been largely forgotten these days.

Octopussy, as far as Roger's Bond films go, got pretty good reviews when it was released. The New York Times wrote - 'George MacDonald Fraser, Richard Maibaum and Michael G. Wilson are responsible for the story and screenplay, which was directed by John Glen, who does much better than he did with For Your Eyes Only. However, the material is markedly better, and the budget seems noticeably larger. Peter Lamont's production design is both extravagant and funny.'

The Washington Post was also in a generous mood and wrote - 'The most striking improvement in Octopussy is the recovery of smoothly coordinated teamwork and entertainment machine maintenance. The mixture of elements that contribute to a satisfying Bond adventure now seems astutely measured again. For example, a cumbersome chase sequence, in which Bond becomes the prey of an elaborate hunting party in an Indian jungle, is finessed with impressive aplomb by an effective throwaway joke--when Bond makes like Tarzan all of a sudden.'

Variety praised the stunts in the film while The Los Angeles Times wrote - 'After all this time, it's amazing that the same old formula still plays: the gadgetry, gorgeous girls, travelogue locales and the shameless double-entendres—in this instance, octo-entendres.' Even the notoriously hard to please Gene Siskel in The Chicago Tribune, who usually seemed to dislike Roger Moore's Bond films, was rather generous for a change. Siskel opined that Octopussy was "surprisingly entertaining— surprising because in his previous five Bond appearances Roger Moore has always come off as a smug stiff. In Octopussy Moore relaxes a bit and, just as important, his role is subordinated to the film's many and extremely exciting action scenes. Octopussy has the most sustained excitement in a Bond film since You Only Live Twice."

If a 1983 interview he conducted with Starlog for the release of Octopussy is anything to go by, James Bond writer Richard Maibaum wasn't the biggest fan of Roger Moore's Bond. Maibaum felt the films had become too tongue-in-cheek and complained that Roger kept changing lines in the script in favour of his own quips! Most of the critics seemed to be strangely charmed by Octopussy at the time though.

More modern retrospective reviews of the movie seem to be (unfairly in my opinion because Octopussy is a lot of fun) much more negative though. One theme in the 1983 reviews though, and it was perhaps unavoidable given that Roger was now 55, was that the Bond franchise probably need to draw a line under the Roger Moore era and find a younger actor. Roger Moore did a set interview for Entertainment Weekly while shooting Octopussy and seemed to concur with this perception. Roger said that six 007 pictures was more than enough and that he didn't expect play Bond again.

In an interview with Barry Norman to promote Never Say Never Again, Sean Connery said that he felt both him and Roger Moore were too old to play James Bond again and suggested Mel Gibson as the next 007. US Magazine asked its readers in 1983 to vote for who they thought the next James Bond should be. The poll was won by Pierce Brosnan in a landslide with 46% of the vote. In second place with 11% was Lewis Collins. Other names who earned votes from readers were Tom Selleck, Ian Oglivy, and Mel Gibson.

Octopussy made $187.5 million from a $27.5 million budget. This was slightly down on For Your Eyes Only but still perfectly respectable. EON were especially encouraged to see that Octopussy did very well in the United States. In the end, Octopussy made more money than Never Say Never Again - which obviously seemed to justify the decision to get Roger back. Never Say Never Again was released a few months after Octopussy and made about $20 million less. Surprisingly, Never Say Never Again had a bigger budget than Octopussy - which is odd because if you watch the two films Octopussy seems more lavish than Never Say Never Again.

Every fresh script rewrite on Never Say Never Again had to be approved by an insurance company lest it should flout Kevin McClory's strictly defined Bond rights (which permitted to remake Thunderball - NOT make up his own Bond film) and give Cubby Broccoli any fresh legal ammunition. Right up until the week that Never Say Never Again was due to hit cinemas, Cubby Broccoli and EON were still in court trying to block the film's release. Although most Bond fans would probably agree that Never Say Never Again could have been a lot better, it got incredible reviews when it first came out. The Chicago Sun Times likened the return of Connery to a Beatles reunion. Never Say Never Again grossed $160 million from a $36 million budget.

Roger made one other film appearance in 1983 - though he probably shouldn't have bothered. Curse of the Pink Panther was another of Blake Edwards' pointless attempts to keep the Pink Panther series going despite the death of Peter Sellers. In Trail of the Pink Panther, Edwards had utilised unsued footage of the late star but this time Edwards essentially replaces Clouseau with an inept American detective named Clifton Sleigh and played by Ted Wass. Edwards had wanted to cast Dudley Moore or Rowan Atkinson as the new inept detective but Dudley Moore declined the part and the studio would not approve Atkinson because he was only famous in Britain. Wass later became best known as Mayim Bialik's dad on the teen sitcom Blossom.

A number of regulars from the series return for a payday despite the sad absence of Sellers. Herbert Lom as the long suffering Dreyfuss, Burt Kwouk as Clouseau's karate chopping manservant Kato, Robert Loggia as Mafia goon Langois. Roger was a friend and neighbour of Blake Edwards in Switzerland and agreed to appear in the film for a cameo although - as he points out in his book - it was rather embarrassing when Sellers' widows personally expressed their dissatisfaction to him at Edwards trying to continue the series after the death of their former husband. They thought it was in rather bad taste. Roger was hired at a generous $100,000 a day near the end of the Octopussy shoot but, to his and his bank manager's annoyance you'd imagine, they shot his contribution in one day! The film was not a success and the option on Wass to make more Pink Panther films was not taken up. Edwards made one more ill-fated attempt to continue the series with Roberto Benigni in 1993's Son of the Pink Panther. It was the last film Edwards made.

At the end of Octopussy's end credits, the familiar James Bond Will Return coda listed the next film as From a View to a Kill. But who would play Bond in this film? In the preamble to A View To A Kill (as it eventually became) going into production there were vague tabloid rumours that Lewis Collins was back in contention to become 007 but these stories turned out not to have much basis in fact.

"I really don't know if I am in the running," said Lewis Collins in 1984. "I certainly haven't been approached by Broccoli. If they did approach me, I don't know what I would say – it really would depend on what was offered. If I had to sign a seven-year contract I'd probably say 'No' just because I wouldn't want to be that tied down. I certainly wouldn't envy anyone taking over the rôle at this stage, especially if they kept to the same format. They would have to allow the next guy to be himself and bring what he has to offer to the rôle. And then, it would take at least two movies to convince the world you are Bond. Even so, I have to admit it would be fun."

From 1984 to 1988, Lewis Collins made a trilogy of Italian/German action films for the director Antonio Margheriti. Margheriti had directed David Warbeck in his Euro action capers so Collins was basically stepping into Warbeck's shoes. The films were Code Name: Wild Geese, Commando Leopard, and The Commander. These movies are undemanding fun with co-stars like Lee Van Cleef, Klaus Kinski and Ernrst Borgnine. Lewis Collins said he didn't like these movies much and only did them for the money. He was tiring of being typecast as an action man and wanted to do other things.

Some sources contend, without much evidence, that Lewis Collins was in the mix for The Living Daylights (he was only 40 at the time of the Daylights casting so still young enough) in 1986 but his Bond dream never really came close to happening. It seems that ultimately, for whatever reason, Cubby Broccoli didn't actually like Lewis Collins very much - which is a shame. One can't help thinking that Lewis Collins would have been a fun eighties Bond. Picture for a moment Bodie from The Professionals with a much better haircut. You've pretty much got 007 right there!

Meanwhile, Michael Billington's attempts to crack the American market had not gone terribly well. The Quest was axed and Billington had small roles in Magnum and Fantasy Island. In 1984, Billington shot a film called KGB: The Secret War in which he played a KGB sleeper agent. His co-stars included Sally Kellerman and Walter Gotell. Billington beat Timothy Dalton to win the lead in KGB: The Secret War and later joked that he only got the part because he was much cheaper to hire than Tim!

Michael Billington is actually very good in KGB: The Secret War and still looks quite James Bondish. However, Billington also looks like he is starting to get a bit of middle-age spread and becoming a trifle heavy. At 43 his days as a Bond candidate were more or less over. Remarkably, despite being a decade and a half older, Roger Moore had actually outlasted Billington when it came to Bond. By the time the James Bond part was up for grabs again in 1986, Michael Billington was considered too old and no longer a contender. In 1986, Michael Billington appeared in a BBC show called The Collectors about customs and excise officials. This show bombed and only lasted ten episodes. After that Billington seemed to (rather like Lewis Collins) slowly drift out of acting.

1984, the year before Roger Moore's last Bond film was released, saw a number of rumours that Pierce Brosnan was going to be the new Bond. An Australian newspaper published an article in which they said Brosnan had already signed a secret deal to replace Roger. Brosnan had to deny these rumours and even wrote to Cubby Broccoli assuring him that these stories did not originate from him or anyone connected to him. It was pretty obvious though that Pierce Brosnan was now in pole position. People watched his TV show Remington Steele and couldn't help but imagine him as James Bond. The part suddenly seemed to be Brosnan's to lose now.

Roger made a picture called The Naked Face in between his last two Bond films. As he neared the end of his long run as James Bond, Roger was approached by Yoram Globus and Menahem Golan of Cannon Films to discuss making a film together. Cannon Films were thrifty but shrewd low-budget chancers who made a lot of action films in the eighties featuring Charles Bronson and Chuck Norris. However they financed an eclectic range of projects away from action fare and seemed happy enough when Roger suggested that Sidney Sheldon's novel The Naked Face might make a good film.

Understandably perhaps, Roger was eager to do something away from the action genre and play a more vulnerable and normal character for a change. He even persuaded Cannon to allow his old friend Bryan Forbes (director of films like Whistle Down the Wind and The Stepford Wives) to direct the film and adapt the screenplay. A decent cast was assembled besides Roger with Elliott Gould, Rod Steiger and Anne Archer taking supporting roles. Roger's old friend David Hedison also took a part in the film. The Naked Face has Roger as Dr Judd Stevens, a psychoanalyst who becomes the prime suspect when some of his patients start being murdered. When his secretary is killed, Stevens realises that he might be the killer's true target. But what is the motive?

Unfortunately, the production of The Naked Face was not a happy one it seems. Cannon cut the production schedule from twelve to eight weeks and Roger also had to fly from Chicago to England when his mother was taken ill. When he returned to the set and learned that the producers had been angry at Forbes for releasing him to fly to his mother's bedside, Roger was understandably annoyed. Cannon Films and Globus and Golan could get knotted as far as he was concerned. Roger believed The Naked Face was a good film but felt the 18 certificate it was lumbered with wrecked any chances it may have had of finding an audience.

The next Bond film would take its name from a story in an Ian Fleming collection titled For Your Eyes only. George

MacDonald Fraser was asked to come back to write the new film but he was unavailable. Richard Maibaum Michael G Wilson were the old hands tasked with the script in the end. John Glen also returned to direct his third Bond film on the spin. It was also announced that Roger Moore would be back as Bond.

Given Roger's age it was surprising that there wasn't more doubt or uncertainty about his participation in the next film but Cubby, John Glen, and the studio were perfectly happy for Roger to come back - despite his advancing years. Roger was 57 (he was actually 58 by the time shooting wrapped on A View To A Kill) now so it was generally assumed this would be his last movie. It was pretty remarkable that Roger was already 45 when he became Bond but still ended up making a record seven movies!

A View To a Kill began shooting in the summer of 1984. David Bowie was touted for the role of Zorin by Cubby Broccoli but in the end the part was taken by Christopher Walken. Walken was something of a coup to get because he was a highly acclaimed actor. David Bowie later said he thought the script was terrible and that he didn't even like Bond films much anyway. He went off to make the cult classic Labyrinth instead. Sting was also under consideration for the part of Zorin but he apparently wasn't interested either. When a company with a name similar to Zorin (the Zoran Corporation) was discovered in the United States, a disclaimer was added to the start of the film affirming that Zorin was not related to any real-life company.

The singer and actress Grace Jones was cast as May Day after Broccoli saw her in Conan the Destroyer. Grace Jones was allowed to design her own clothes as May Day in A View To A Kill. Roger Moore, if his memoirs are to be believed, didn't get on very well with Grace Jones. 'I'm afraid my diplomatic charm was stretched to the limit. Every day in her dressing room - which was adjacent to mine - she played very loud music. I was not a fan of heavy metal. One day I snapped. I marched into her room, pulled the plug and then went back to my room, picked up a chair and flung it at the wall.'

The then boyfriend of Grace Jones, a certain Dolph Lundgren, can be seen briefly in A View To A Kill as a KGB heavy. Lundgren would get his big break soon after with Rocky IV - where he played the hulking steroid enhanced Soviet boxing villain Ivan Drago. One of Barbara Broccoli's jobs on A View To A Kill was to make sure that Grace Jones got to the set on time. This was no easy task because Grace Jones hated early mornings. It is believed that Barbara's diplomatic skills were considerably enhanced by the experience of sharing a car with a grumpy Grace Jones at the crack of dawn!

Priscilla Presley and Sharon Stone were considered for the part of Stacey Sutton but in the end it went to Tanya Roberts - fresh from her role in Sheena: Queen of the Jungle.

Roger Moore would later quip that he knew it was time to quit Bond when he realised he was old enough to be Tanya's father. Tanya Roberts played Julie Rogers in the final season of the television series Charlie's Angels. It has been reported that Priscilla Presley couldn't do A View To A Kill because of her contract on the soap opera Dallas (which she was appearing at the time) but other stories say she wasn't interested anyway. Priscilla Presley showed a good knack for deadpan comedy four years later when she appeared in The Naked Gun with Leslie Nielson.

Bo Derek is also alleged to have been considered for the part of Stacey Sutton. This has some credence because Bo Derek was later one of the celebrity guests at the premiere of A View To A Kill. She was one of the big sex symbols of her era and clearly had the looks to be in a Bond film but it was most likely her acting ability which made EON think twice. One could argue though that Tanya Roberts wasn't exactly Meryl Streep either! John Glen later said that he thought Tanya Roberts was the most beautiful of the Bond Girls he directed. Cubby Broccoli apparently got the idea to cast Tanya Roberts in a Bond film after watching her in the 1982 sword and sorcery caper The Beastmaster.

Patrick Macnee was cast as Bond's contact Tibbet in the film. Roger Moore and Macnee were old friends and had appeared in Sherlock Holmes in New York and The Sea Wolves together. Anya Amasova was supposed to cameo in A View To A Kill but Barbara Bach didn't want to appear. The character was therefore changed to become Pola Ivanova, a KGB agent known to Bond. Maryam D'Abo tested for this part but was deemed to be too young. John Glen kept her in mind though and she would appear in the next Bond film as the female lead (by that time Roger Moore had obviously made way for Timothy Dalton). In the end, Fiona Fullerton was cast as Pola. Fiona Fullerton was well known to EON because she would sometimes act in the auditions for prospective Bond actors.

It was planned for Felix Leiter to be in A View To A Kill but in the end this idea was axed and Leiter became the character played by David Yip in the movie. Two time Bond Girl Maud Adams is a background extra in A View To A Kill. She visited the San Francisco set to say hello to Roger Moore and so they put her in a crowd scene. Lois Maxwell made her last appearance as as Miss Moneypenny in this movie. It would obviously have been impossible to retain Lois after Roger left because she would have been considerably older than the new Bond actor. Robert Brown and Desmond Llewelyn were luckier though and continued as M and Q respectively in the Timothy Dalton films. Desmond Llewelyn would also appear in three Brosnan Bond movies before bowing out of the franchise in 1999.

Duran Duran nabbed the Bond theme when John Taylor approached Bond producer Cubby Broccoli and asked why they didn't let a more current act have a bash at a 007 song to shake things up somewhat. To the surprise of everyone (including John Barry), Broccoli permitted Duran Duran to have a go themselves and it all worked out fine in the end. Duran Duran's A View to a Kill was the first Bond theme to hit

No. 1 on the Billboard Top 100. The score is interesting because John Barry allows for some modernity so you get a vague sense of transition and modern (eighties) flourishes. It's a double edged sword of course and makes some of the music sound a little cheesy here and there but it's still a lavish and highly entertaining score in the best Barry tradition. Romantic and exciting with some trademark brass and subtle string arpeggios.

There was a bit of a disaster during the production of A View To A Kill when the 007 Stage at Pinewood Studios burned down. Cubby Broccoli mulled this disaster over for a moment and then ordered it to be rebuilt! It was renamed Albert R. Broccoli's 007 Stage when it reopened at the start of 1985. Roger Moore was on hand for a special ceremony. The snowboarding sequence in the PTS took six weeks to complete and was performed by a 22 year-old American snowboarding expert named Steve Link. Link got a funny letter from Roger Moore to thank him for his work on the movie. Roger wrote - 'Many thanks for the splendid work you did. It looks absolutely great on the screen - I don't think I have ever been quite so brave.'

A View To A Kill is the seventh and final film to feature Roger Moore as James Bond and the fourteenth entry in the franchise. The film is not widely regarded to be one of the strongest entries in the series and often crops up near the bottom of Bond fan lists. A View To A Kill is very entertaining in parts but does feel like the series coasting along while it braces itself for some inevitable changes. A View To A Kill's plot is essentially an update of Goldfinger with Silicon Valley replacing Fort Knox.

James Bond investigates wealthy microchip industrialist Max Zorin (Christopher Walken) in the film and stumbles upon a scheme that proposes to flood oil wells along the San Andreas fault in California, set off explosives and destroy Silicon Valley. Such a scheme would of course make Zorin's business considerably more lucrative and unique. Zorin is basically

Auric Goldfinger but with microchips replacing gold. Along the way we get the usual stunts, chases, double entendres, beautiful women, humour, one-liners, sadism, and most of the general nonsense and fun that you'd expect from a Roger Moore James Bond film.

The film begins with an enjoyable pre-credits ski chase set in Siberia which sees Bond involved in some snowboarding action as he recovers a microchip from a dead 00 agent which is resistant to electromagnetic interference. The inclusion of a version of California Girls on the soundtrack is though unnecessary (as is the iceberg submarine!) but the essential fun of the sequence - Bond outsmarting some Soviet troops in the snow with some nifty stunts - remains and John Barry's score is wonderful with great action cues. California Girls is a mistake because it suddenly turns a tense and exciting sequence into a comedy sequence. They should have just let John Barry's music be the backdrop to the entire PTS.

John Barry's main theme, a poppy rabble rouser performed by Duran, Duran also works very well although Maurice Binder's titles are not quite up to his usual standards and seem to make extensive use of luminous paint! After the usual M scenes there is some pleasant location work at Ascot with Q and Moneypenny enjoying a day at the races as Bond and company watch Zorin. Both Moore and Lois Maxwell bowed out after A View To A Kill and it's nice to see them all having one more adventure together before being put out to pasture.

There are of course also several big action set-pieces in A View To A Kill, including a chase up the Eiffel Tower, skydiving and much carnage in Paris as Bond steals a car and destroys it - and most of the French capital it seems! "May I remind you," Says M. "That this operation was to be conducted discreetly. All it took was six million Francs in damages and penalties for violating most of the Napoleonic Code." There are some spectacular car stunts in this sequence and May Day's jump off the top of the Eiffel Tower is a memorable moment.
We are introduced to two interesting additions to the cast

somewhere around this point. Good old Patrick Macnee as Sir Godfrey Tibbett, an MI6 contact of Bond, and Grace Jones as May Day, Zorin's bodyguard or 'henchwoman'. Macnee doesn't have a huge role but he works very nicely with Roger Moore in scenes set at Zorin's lavish French estate where the duo go undercover and he pretends to be Bond's butler. You do care what happens to the character of Tibbett - which is to the credit of Macnee.

The casting of Grace Jones was bold - although some felt her character didn't quite live up to the hype upon the original release of A View To A Kill. Personally I thought it was a nice twist to cast a woman as the assistant/henchman and while Grace Jones is no Katherine Hepburn when it comes to snapping out dialogue she does have a very striking appearance and presence that works very well in a Bond film. One thing I do feel is that the old Bond films, even the eighties ones made by the much derided John Glen, had a sense of style and weird sort of natural scope that the more recent Bond films lack. A View To A Kill, for all its faults, is undeniably a very stylish film. The Paris scenes and Zorin's stables/estate bear this out.

The piece of casting that perhaps hasn't endured quite as well is that of the late Tanya Roberts as geologist Stacey Sutton. Tanya is closer to Britt Eklund than Diana Rigg in the mythical pantheon of Bond girls. Elsewhere, Walter Gotell makes a welcome return as General Gogol and Fiona Fullerton has a brief cameo as Pola Ivanova - a sultry Russian agent who shares a hot tub - and some suggestive banter - with Bond. "The bubbles tickle my... Tchaikovsky!" The film could probably have lived without some of this extra silliness at times. Roger is plainly getting a bit long in the tooth to be sharing a hot tub with Fiona Fullerton! Alison Doody also makes her mark as Jenny Flex. I sometimes miss the days when every name in a Bond film was some sort of innuendo!

What else is there to enjoy in A View To A Kill? There is a big fire-engine chase through San Francisco which is enjoyable if a bit overlong and a well staged mine flooding sequence. It was a nice touch to give Zorin a distinctive airship to travel in - lending an air of grace and eccentricity to the character and setting up the climax of the film on top of the Golden Gate Bridge - which I absolutely love, especially when John Barry's music kicks in. Zorin's airship is also used for a nice Goldfinger joke/reference and update of Mr Solo's "Pressing engagement."

Probably the best thing A View To A Kill has going for it is Christopher Walken as Zorin. "Intuitive improvisation is the secret of genius," says old Max. In the Bond films that have followed A View To A Kill, perhaps only Robert Davi as Sanchez in Licence To Kill has provided a villain to rank alongside Max Zorin. Walken is eccentric, stylish, sadistic and seems to be having a lot of fun. Note his psychotic laugh as he guns down his own mineworkers!

Roger Moore is also good in what would be his final appearance in the franchise. Sure, he's knocking on and probably should have bowed out after For Your Eyes Only in 1981 but he still looks stylish and handsome in the film and brings his usual sense of fun to the part. Much is made of the fact that Roger Moore supposedly looks ancient in A View to A Kill and is alleged to have had a facelift before the movie - which some think makes him look weird. I don't concur with this theory myself. Roger had cosmetic surgery to remove his facial mole before the movie and he seems to have some work done on his eyes but I think Roger actually looks better in this movie than he did in Octopussy. I think Roger looks fine in A View To A Kill.

Roger was always good at those little scenes where Bond mocks the villain at some swanky function and lets him know that he's onto him. In A View To A Kill, Moore has a few good bits like this with Zorin and some other nice moments. "Brilliant," says Bond seriously after Zorin has shot somebody. "I'm almost speechless with admiration." Roger is surprisingly good sometimes when one of his Bond scripts requires him to play it straight for a moment.

A View To A Kill is decent, underrated 007 fun. It has too much humour for its own good at times and could have been trimmed a little in length I think to give it a little more pace. The iceberg sub, the Beach Boys, and Pola Ivanova are not essential parts of the film and could have been lost but for me A View To A Kill - while having weaknesses - also has a lot going for it. It might not be the best James Bond film ever made but that doesn't automatically make it a bad film. A View To A Kill has a weird defence mechanism in a way as the consensus remembers it as a terrible film but, mostly, it's perfectly watchable and amusing to modern eyes with good production values and a stirring John Barry score.

CHAPTER TEN - THE END OF AN ERA

The premiere for A View To A Kill took place on 22 May 1985 at San Francisco's Palace of Fine Arts. It was unusual for a Bond premiere to take place outside of Britain. The British premiere was held on 12 June 1985 at the Odeon Leicester Square cinema in London. This Royal premiere was attended by Prince Charles and Princess Diana. The marketing for the movie included the usual brochures, toys, trading cards, alarm clocks, and food brand deals.

Roger Moore was his usual jokey self when he did the rounds of the chat show studios to promote the film. Roger said it was tough to come up with new ideas and stunts to put in a Bond film these days. He was even asked what he thought about the rumours that Pierce Brosnan was going to replace him. Roger, ever the diplomat, said he thought Pierce would be great. Roger was STILL being asked about Never Say Never Again in interviews but he had the perfect response because he simply told interviewers that he had never actually watched the film and so had no opinion on it!

A View To A Kill was unusual in that it was the first Roger Moore Bond film (or Bond film period) to get an official computer game in the form of a 1985 Domark game titled (you guessed it) A View To A Kill. This game must rank as one of my most disappointing gaming experiences on the Commodore 64. A game based on a Bond film! This must be good right? Wrong! A View To A Kill has three different sections which are essentially like minigames. All of these sections are tedious.

The first section in the game has you driving through Paris as Bond chasing May Day. Sounds great right? Unfortunately this must be the worst driving section of any game I have ever played. It's slow, graphically awful, and Paris consists of a series of brick walls. Half the screen in the Paris section is top down and the top half of the screen is first perspective. The 3D scrolls with all the speed of a limping snail!

Next is City Hall where you must escape as the building is on fire. You have to get various locked doors open. This second section is as boring a the first. It's a side-on puzzle section where your have to find objects to progress and must also douse the fire with buckets of water. James Bond is depicted by a blocky stick man figure. In the third section of the game you run around Zorin's mines - basically rubbish platform action!

The poor graphics and thrown together nature of this game are inexcusable given that it is an official Bond game. The C64 was capable of smooth and fluid animations and fast scrolling (look at games like Impossible Mission and Super Cycle) so it is a shame that none of these qualities were apparent in A View To A Kill's computer game. A View To A Kill is absolutely abysmal with dreadful crude graphics and a complete lack of compulsive gameplay.

Zzap64 magazine awarded A View To A Kill's computer game just 36%. What was most disappointing about the game is that it was heavily hyped. As far as the C64 went, the games to approach with some degree of caution were the licenced games. Companies would get the rights to some popular movie or television show and inevitably the game they knocked up with said licence would be terrible. That cover art would always lure you in though. This was clearly the case with A View To A Kill. The box looked great but the actual game was hopeless.

As for the actual movie, A View To A Kill met with a dismal critical reception when the reviews started coming in. 'A View to a Kill,' wrote the New York Times, 'should be no surprise to anyone who has seen the other recent Bond films with Mr Moore, and no strain on the intelligence or memory of anyone else. It does hold the attention, in a what-won't-they-think-of-next? manner, while under way. It's entirely forgettable a moment later.'

Variety also seemed bored by the film. 'Director John Glen, who previously directed For Your Eyes Only, has not found the right balance between action and humour to make the production dangerous fun. Walken, too, the product of a mad Nazi scientist's genetic experiments, is a bit wimpy by Bond villain standards. With hair colored an unnaturally yellow he seems more effete than deadly. As for Roger Moore, making his seventh appearance as Bond, he is right about half the time, he still has the suave and cool for the part, but on occasion he looks a bit old for the part and his coy womanizing seems dated when he does. Other instances when the film strives to stake its claim to the rock video audience backfire and miscalculate the appeal of the material.'

Pauline Kael of The New Yorker gave the film both barrels and said - "The James Bond series has had its bummers, but nothing before in the class of A View to a Kill. You go to a Bond picture expecting some style or, at least, some flash, some lift; you don't expect the dumb police-car crashes you get here. You do see some ingenious daredevil feats, but they're crowded together and, the way they're set up, they don't give you the irresponsible, giddy tingle you're hoping for."

The Washington Post was also uncomplimentary and spent most of its review talking about how old Roger Moore was. 'At the finale of A View to a Kill, James Bond (Roger Moore) dangles from a blimp, an almost painfully appropriate metaphor for the adventure series that is now bloated, slow moving and at the end of its rope. It`s not double-oh-seven anymore, but double-oh-seventy, the best argument yet for the mandatory retirement age.'

Newsweek also seemed to dislike A View To A Kill. 'In his seventh film as James Bond, Roger Moore seems tired out. A View To A Kill succumbs to all the cliches and conventions associated with its forerunners but lacks the spirit to compete. Hollywood Bond productions have come to sacrifice urbanity for exotic stunts and fast action. With the exception of an ingenious plot idea and the unconventional beauty Grace Jones as the Amazonian May Day, the film comes off as an insipid foil for a couple of brilliant stunt sequences. In his seventh movie as James Bond, Rog is looking less like a chap with a license to kill than a gent with an application to retire. Moore is an extremely engaging fellow and an admirable professional, but when he turns on that famous quizzical smile, his facial muscles look as if they're lifting weights.'

It wasn't all doom and gloom though. There were a FEW decent reviews. When people do their Bond film rankings these days, A View To A Kill tends to rank near the bottom but the film had its fans though. John Brosnan in Starburst called it the best of the Roger Moore Bonds. The Canadian critic Lawrence O'Toole was also a big fan and wrote of A View To A Kill - 'Of all the modern formulas in the movie industry, the James Bond series is among the most pleasurable and durable. Lavish with their budgets, the producers also bring a great deal of craft, wit and a sense of fun to the films.

'Agent 007 is like an old friend who an audience meets for drinks every two years or so; he regales them with tall tales, winking all the time. The 14th and newest Bond epic, A View to a Kill, is an especially satisfying encounter. Opening with a breathtaking ski chase in Siberia, A View to a Kill is the fastest Bond picture yet. Its pace has the precision of a Swiss watch and the momentum of a greyhound on the track. There is a spectacular chase up and down the Eiffel Tower and through Paris streets, which Bond finishes in a severed car on just two wheels. But none of the action prepares the viewer for the heart-stopping climax with Zorin's dirigible tangled in the cables on top of San Francisco's Golden Gate Bridge.'

Fans of A View To A Kill did not though include Roger Moore. He later said it was his least favourite out of his Bond pictures. "I was horrified on the last Bond I did. Whole slews of sequences where Christopher Walken was machine-gunning hundreds of people. I said 'That wasn't Bond, those weren't

Bond films.' It stopped being what they were all about. You didn't dwell on the blood and the brains spewing all over the place." A View To A Kill made $152.4 million. This was a respectable tally given the negative reviews. The film struggled somewhat in North America because it opened against Rambo: First Blood Part II. The action cinema landscape was changing fast and a Bond reboot was plainly on the cards.

In the wake of A View To A Kill there would be no more drama regarding Roger's future participation in the franchise. Roger announced at the end of 1985 that he had retired from the Bond role and was standing down. Roger later took issue with Cubby Broccoli's assertion that he gave Roger the heave-ho after A View To A Kill for being too old. Roger Moore maintained he had in fact retired himself from the series and no one asked him to leave. It is sometimes reported that the next Bond film was originally written in a generic way lest Roger Moore should come back again. There doesn't seem to be much evidence for this. In fact, The Living Daylights was originally conceived as a prequel featuring a young Bond at the start of his career. There was never too much danger of a sixty-something Roger Moore coming back to make an eighth film.

The James Bond series naturally went on way beyond Roger Moore. Moore had taken over the role of Bond at a tricky time but he had steered the franchise through the seventies and half of the eighties and proved that someone other than Sean Connery could put their stamp on the part. It is easy to underestimate what Roger Moore did but it should not be downplayed. At the time of Live and Let Die only one actor other than Connery had played Bond and he only lasted for ONE film. Roger lasted for SEVEN films - a tally that is unlikely ever to be matched (especially these days when EON seem to take several years to even get ONE of these films out).

EON, as was expected, replaced Roger in 1986 with Pierce Brosnan. However, when Brosnan's television show Remington Steel was reactivated to cash in on the 007 publicity, Brosnan had to depart because Cubby Broccoli had no intention of sharing his Bond actor with a TV show. Brosnan would have to wait until 1994 to finally land Bond for good. Timothy Dalton was chosen to replace Brosnan in Daylights and became the fourth official Bond actor. Dalton represented the fresh start that the franchise needed. His moody and serious Bond was a complete about turn from the Roger Moore years and The Living Daylights is fairly highly regarded these days - even if it didn't get ecstatic reviews back in 1987.

Timothy, to his credit, did Bond HIS way and was completely different to Roger. The box-office for The Living Daylights was decent enough but, as we know, the Dalton era hit a fork in the road a few years later and was sunk by litigation and the lukewarm box-office of Licence To Kill. Dalton was more appreciated by Bond fans than general audiences whereas with Roger you could argue it was actually the other way around. Here's the interesting thing about the reviews for The Living Daylights though. A number of reviewers commented that Dalton didn't have the wit or suaveness of Roger Moore!

At the start of Roger's tenure, critics grumbled that he wasn't Sean Connery. Now the critics - who were notoriously sniffy towards Roger when he played Bond - actually seemed to be missing him! Roger had played Bond for so many films that it was difficult to shake off the large shadow he cast over the franchise and accept someone else as Bond. Pierce Brosnan would later say that when he played James Bond he always felt adrift somewhere in the middle of the template set by Connery and Moore. That was a common complaint of the Brosnan films - a confusion of tone. They could never quite decide if they wanted Pierce to be Roger Moore or Sean Connery. Roger Moore's legacy was clearly much greater than anyone ever really gave him credit for at the time.

After completing his last Bond film, Roger seemed to drift away from acting to the point where he seemed almost retired at times. His main focus was on his duties as a UNICEF Goodwill Ambassador. Roger did return in the 1990s though.

Some of the films he appeared in were truly awful (Fire, Ice and Dynamite, Bullseye!, Spice World) but there was one shining light with Bed & Breakfast. Bed & Breakfast was produced by Jack Schwartzman, who also produced the renegade Sean Connery Bond film Never Say Never Again (which went up against Roger's Octopussy in 1983). Further James Bond connections with Bed & Breakfast? The director Robert Ellis Miller had recently directed Timothy Dalton in Hawks and Brenda Starr.

Although Bed & Breakfast has been almost completely forgotten it deserved a somewhat better fate as it's a very charming little film at times and one of the best pictures Roger featured in outside of Bond. It was shot in 1989 and given a limited release three years later in 1992 - which probably explains its relative obscurity. Bed & Breakfast revolves around three generations of women who run a struggling guest house in a picturesque coastal town in Maine. The earthy Ruth (Colleen Dewhurst) is bored and seeks some excitement in her autumn years while her sensitive daughter-in-law Claire (Talia Shire) is a widow suffering from the humiliation caused by a warts and all biography which suggested that her late politician husband was less than faithful to her.

Last but not least is Claire's daughter Cassie (Nina Siemaszko) - who suffers from the usual emotional ups and downs and strops of teenage life and wants to be a musician despite the pressure Claire puts on her to pursue a more academic life and maybe go into politics like her father. One day the women find a bloodied bedraggled stranger washed up on the beach and after some debate allow him to recover in their house. The stranger is a suave Englishman (played by Roger naturally) who they come to know as Adam. Despite the initial protests of Claire, they allow him to stay to do odd jobs around the house and he begins to have a profound effect on their lives. Adam had a dodgy past though - which threatens to catch up with him.

There isn't much of a plot to Bed & Breakfast and not an awful lot happens but it doesn't really matter in the end. The lovely seascapes are the star of the film and give Bed & Breakfast a lot of charm. Lighthouses, rocky beaches. It's one of those films where you wouldn't mind entering the screen for an hour or so to wander around Purple Rose of Cairo style. Roger looks great in the film, better in fact than he did in his last couple of Bond adventures. The end of those long days at Pinewood shooting Bond films looks like it did him the world of good. Roger made a few other films in the end. The Quest (which is watchable enough) with Jean Clade Van Damme, Boat Trip (a ribald comedy which is not worth your time), and three television movies - of which only The Man Who Wouldn't Die is worth watching.

Roger was not just a UNICEF Goodwill Ambassador in his last years. He was also an Ambassador for the James Bond franchise. And what a class act Roger was in Bond themed documentaries and interviews. In 2005, Daniel Craig was announced as the new Bond and got a terrible reception in the press. Who did EON get to come in and do some firefighting? That's right - Roger Moore. Roger defended Daniel Craig in the media and talked about what a good actor Craig was. Roger was typically classy in talking up Craig and being completely loyal to EON and Cubby's heirs.

Modern Bond retrospectives tend to, for reasons that escape me, almost completely dismiss Roger's tenure as James Bond. He is frequently called the 'worst' Bond and his movies are dismissed as Carry On style romps. Roger would even make light of this himself. The truth is though that Roger was a great Bond. Sure, he maybe made a couple of films too many and the comedic elements of his films sometimes got out of hand but the Roger years constitute the most fun era of Bond.

If you sit down and watch one of Roger's Bond films you are guaranteed to have a good undemanding time. Fun and humour is an important component of the Bond franchise and when you forget these elements you end up with grim generic films like Quantum of Solace or No Time To Die. Roger

Moore's Bond, by contrast, is pure Christmas Day afternoon. John Barry, Ken Adam, Lewis Gilbert, Carly Simon, crazy stunts, quips, Caroline Munro in a helicopter, underwater bases, Jaws, Jane Seymour, the Lotus, parachutes, jet planes, space battles, crocodiles, ski chases, casinos, tuxedos, double-entendres. The Roger Moore era of Bond wasn't terrible or embarrassing. It was fantastic!

CHAPTER ELEVEN - MOORE NEVER LESS

In order to asses the Roger Moore era of Bond it might be a good idea to go back to the start to explore why he was cast and what the alternatives were. The first non-Connery Bond, George Lazenby, was not overwhelmingly accepted purely because he wasn't Sean Connery. If we dismiss the unrealistic dreams of United Artists to cast a Hollywood star like Steve McQueen or Clint Eastwood as Bond, this meant that EON had to find a British actor in 1972 who was capable of keeping the ship afloat through the 1970s. What they basically needed was someone of reasonable stature. Someone who was already quite well known and a professional experienced actor (Lazenby, though good in OHMSS, was obviously not a seasoned actor - in fact, he wasn't an actor at all).

The British actors EON mulled over for the part of James Bond in Live and Let Die were John Richardson, David Warbeck, Patrick Mower, Julian Glover, John Ronane, William Gaunt, Jeremy Brett, and Michael Billington. It's difficult to imagine that any of these actors would have been a better or more popular custodian of the Bond franchise than Roger Moore was. Can anyone really picture William Gaunt as James Bond? The most plausible alternative to Roger was clearly Billington - who run Roger very close in the end. From all that we know, Cubby Broccoli and Harry Saltzman would have been happy to cast Michael Billington as James Bond.

Though he never really became a star or that well known, Billington was actually a very competent actor and he had a classic Milk Tray man sort of look which would have been perfect for Bond. He was a very viable Bond candidate in the 1970s and early 1980s. Billington had quite a grumpy, moody sort of acting persona though. He would have been a tougher and more sober and solemn sort of Bond than Roger. This would doubtless have endeared him more to purists than Roger but was it what the franchise needed at the time? Could a Michael Billington Bond have delivered the quips like Roger and been as much fun? Highly doubtful.

Would the hiring of Billington also have made the writers constrictive in what type of film they produced? You could imagine Michael Billington in Live and Let Die or The Man with the Golden Gun but you can't really imagine him so readily in The Spy Who Loved Me or Moonraker. Roger had the screen presence to keep his head above water in huge gadget laden extravaganzas but would Billington? Billington's lack of profile might also have been a problem.

Audiences were accepting of Roger in 1973 because they already knew him. He was Simon Templar and Lord Brett Sinclair. Billington, despite his television credits, would have been seen as another unknown like Lazenby - especially outside of Britain where most people wouldn't have seen him in anything. I like Michael Billington and think he would have been a good Bond. It's a shame he didn't get to do a couple. But the sensible and pragmatic decision was clearly to cast Roger Moore. Roger was 6'2, handsome, and even still youthful looking in 1972. Roger was the perfect person to get Bond through the 1970s. He laid the foundation for the franchise to carry on into eternity.

Roger's first two Bond films failed to strike gold. They were both decent entries in the Bond canon but didn't set the world alight. They were inconsistent in tone and featured topical elements that would date them quickly. Roger was fine without being great. Ok without being terrible. If anything the series was sliding into an abyss of apathy. Far from saving the series, it looked like Roger would be the man at the helm when the ship ran aground. After The Man with The Golden Gun stalled at the box-office and met with bland reviews, it seemed like James Bond was almost finished.

When Saltzman sold out his share in the franchise and left Cubby Broccoli as the sole producer the writing was on the wall. But a curious thing happened that would lay the ground for the future of Bond. Cubby took this as a personal challenge. He resolved to make the biggest Bond ever and restore 007 to his former glory. The Spy Who Loved Me, a ludicrously fantastical and lavishly produced epic, finally cemented Roger as Bond and revived the franchise. Not only was the seventies assured but the eighties now looked certain to see James Bond too. At the age of 49, Roger Moore had done the impossible: a non-Connery Bond had proved popular and viable. Cubby too had proved he could go it alone.

Roger did all that was asked of him as Bond - including probably saving a franchise. It was the arrival of Lewis Gilbert which enabled Roger to hit his stride as Bond. Gilbert knew how to play to Roger's strengths much more than Guy Hamilton. Although lighter in tone and not appealing to all Bond fans, Moore did offer his own distinctive take on the character - which is all any actor can do, regardless of reactions. Moore Bond's mixture of humour, suaveness, encyclopedic knowledge and occasional ruthlessness was important enough to EON for him to make more films than any other Bond actor. They didn't keep inviting him back because he was unpopular! As much as any other actor Roger Moore reshaped 007 to suit his own distinctive personality; adventurous, funny, assured, sophisticated, urbane and uniquely British.

One of the frequent knocks on Roger Moore is that his Bond couldn't punch his way out of a wet paper bag. We should remember that Moore didn't benefit from the all action editing of Peter Hunt like Connery and Lazenby but he had his moments. His fight with Sandor in The Spy Who Loved Me and the punch-up in the belly dancer's room in The Man With The Golden Gun are examples of Moore being able to punch his way out of trouble when the scriptwriters deemed it necessary. The Spy Who Loved Me and Moonraker were huge OTT epics in the vein of Thunderball and You Only Live Twice a decade earlier. Moore's Bond was a solid anchor in these films and his approach to the character opened up the possibility of these films being produced.

In a long running series like James Bond, different approaches should be taken and a few grandly produced fantastical adventures are all part of the mix. Under the Roger Moore era we (enjoyably) saw the return of the epic James Bond film. Unlike some other Bond actors, Roger also seemed happy to talk about his James Bond days, offering a respectful insight laced with self-deprecation. He, more than anyone, amusingly downplayed his contribution to the series!

Here's the thing too. Roger Moore was always a better actor than either he or critics ever gave him credit for. If you don't think Roger Moore can act then go and watch the film The Man Who Haunted Himself. Roger even has some nice 'acting' moments in the Bond films - not that anyone noticed them. The heart to heart with Melina in the snow in For Your Eyes Only and emerging rattled and sweaty from the centrifuge in Moonraker. When he was asked to play a scene 'straight' Roger was always perfectly adept at doing this.

Clearly though, it was humour that Roger brought the most to Bond. No James Bond actor was quicker with a quip than Roger Moore. While this may have gone overboard at times Moore's films are still a blast to watch today because of a sense of fun that seemed to fit the seventies. It's hard to imagine Michael Billington as a serious, tough as nails Bond enduring through the seventies and beyond but Roger Moore seemed to be the right man in the right place at the right time.

We should also remember that the first 'Roger Moore style' James Bond film was actually called Diamonds Are Forever and starred Sean Connery! It's not as if all the Bond films had dramatic chamber pieces before Roger came along and made the franchise silly! The Spy Who Loved Me and Moonraker are clearly inspired by the grand scale escapism of You Only Live Twice. The Connery and Moore films are not as far apart as lazy retrospectives would have you believe.

I find that the seven films Roger Moore made stand up surprisingly well today. If you take, for example, the Pierce

Brosnan films, they all seem to morph into one another after GoldenEye and aren't especially memorable. The same is sort of true when it comes to the Daniel Craig films. The Craig films after Casino Royale seem to be endlessly mining an increasingly redundant and tiresome theme (Bond is depressed, miserable, heartbroken, retired, sad, presumed dead, etc) and often forget to supply us with the requisite humour and fun we expect from a Bond film.

The films that Roger Moore made though are all sort of distinct and have their own personality. Live and Let Die is the voodoo Blaxsploitation one. The Man with the Golden Gun is arguably a little on the bland side but you always remember Christopher Lee and Nick Nack and the exotic Far East locations. The Spy Who Loved Me is endlessly memorable and the same can be said, for better or for worse, of Moonraker. For Your Eyes Only is also impossible to forget because it's the one where they toned down the gadgets but still had a disco score! Octopussy will always be remembered for the Acrostar jet PTS and A View To A Kill is the one with Grace Jones and the Paris mayhem.

This sort of direct association is not so easy with some of the later Bond films. What makes Spectre lodge in the memory? What makes The World Is Not Enough lodge in the memory? Well, some things for sure and these movies have their fans but the answer to the question is not a lot. The World Is Not Enough has a nice boat chase PTS but thereafter is a lot more difficult to remember. Some of these later Bond movies feel a trifle colourless to me compared to the Moore years - where the budget would fill the screen and John Barry was usually supplying the music. Bond escaping from the crocs in Live and Let Die or parachuting off the mountain in The Spy Who Loved Me, well, these are classic Bond moments from any era - not just the Moore years.

The era of Roger's Bond was not everyone's cup of tea but it was very distinctive. Despite the brickbats which continue to tediously head in the direction of Roger's Bond films I don't personally think any of them are clunkers. A clunker, in the context of Bond, would be something like Die Another Day or Quantum of Solace. Look, I know QoS probably has its fans but that film is like watching watching the rushes of an uncompleted movie! I like all the Roger Bond films to varying degrees. None of them are clunkers to me.

I enjoy Live and Let Die's funky early seventies atmosphere and horror flourishes just fine. I will concede that The Man with the Golden Gun is not the most memorable of Bond films but it isn't outrageously bad. In fact, the locations and Christopher Lee's polished presence make it perfectly watchable. The Spy Who Loved Me is easily in my top four or five Bond and a classic as far as I'm concerned. This had most of what you could want from a Bond film and is full of terrific stunts and wit. Roger Moore was never better than The Spy Who Loved Me. He looks great in the film and is suave and funny. I don't understand how anyone can watch The Spy Who Loved Me and say that Roger Moore was a terrible Bond! Roger is awesome in this film.

Moonraker is definitely an acquired taste but I love the wondrous lavish absurdity of this film and the way it takes the Roger Moore/Lewis Gilbert version of Bond to the absolute height of preposterous fantasy. Sure, Moonraker is TOO much in the end but what an incredible piece of filmmaking it is at times. In terms of box-office and exposure, the latter half of the 1970s was the absolute peak of Roger's Bond. He was in his pomp as 007.

I find For Your Eyes Only to be a trifle overrated by Bond fans but it's still an interesting and well made film and notable for the way it eschews the excesses of the Moore era. For Your Eyes Only is the first film where Roger threatens to become Grandpa Bond and is clearly starting to look too old to be around with twentysomething Bond Girls. Had he bowed out after Moonraker or For Your Eyes Only, I suspect that all the retrospective criticism about Roger being too old in his Bond films would be far less audible these days. It was really Roger in Octopussy and A View To A Kill where his age was all too apparent. These two movies forever enshrined Roger as the 'Geriatric Bond' for future generations of lazy pop culture commentators. Here's the thing though. I actually think Roger's age makes A View To A Kill more memorable! I think he looks fine in that film.

Roger's age as Bond was always more pronounced when they put him in casual clothes for scenes. This is illustrated by For Your Eyes Only and A View To A kill. Roger has some casual ski/winter clobber in the former and actually sports a tracksuit at one point in the latter! You should really keep Roger Moore's Bond in a suit or tuxedo as much as you can. There's a double standard with this ageism because Daniel Craig was 51 in No Time To Die and looked rather craggy and clapped-out in parts of that film and yet his age was not much of an issue when that movie came out. No one refers to Daniel Craig as the Geriatric Bond just because he looked a bit past it at the end of his tenure!

As far as the artistic merit of Roger's last two (and unnecessary as far as many people seem to think) Bond films go, I think Octopussy is a lot of fun (if a trifle too silly for its own good at times) and I'm one of those strange people who has always quite enjoyed A View To A kill and have no idea why it seems to be so reviled. The only conclusion to draw from all of this is that I enjoy the Roger Moore era - warts and all. The films made with Roger were, for me personally, fun and entertaining and full of great Bond moments.

Roger was a class act throughout his tenure, delivering karate chops and quips in his inimitable style. Roger's Bond is effortlessly stylish in Live and Let Die and though he was creaking a bit near the end he was always good value and always fun. When people complain these days about a new Bond film taking itself too seriously or being too miserable their antidote is always the same. They want more fun and humour. They want more outlandish escapism. They want Bond to just be an agent who enjoys his job and goes around the world on a mission. They don't want angst or pretentious drama. You could argue that the real subtext of this yearning - not that anyone would admit to it - is that they want the films to be more like the Roger Moore era!

I would concur with this desire. I don't want the next Bond film to be like Moonraker or Octopussy. I don't even want it to be like The Spy Who Loved Me. The Bond franchise has to do its own thing and look to the future. But the wit, fun, unforgettable stunts, escapism, cheekiness, eye-popping production design, and wondrous music of the Roger Moore era, well, we definitely need to see MORE of this in Bond films going forward - especially after fifteen long years of gloomy Daniel Craig pictures.

So, yes, I am an unashamed fan of Roger Moore's James Bond. Roger was a fantastic Bond and his 007 films are still, whatever their individual flaws, endlessly watchable and entertaining. I am never going to sit down on Christmas Day afternoon and watch No Time To Die. I'm not even going to sit down on Christmas Day afternoon and watch Skyfall. I would happily though watch any of Roger's films - especially The Spy Who Loved Me, Moonraker, and Live and Let Die. What exactly was Roger's contribution to Bond? His contribution was to show that someone other than Sean Connery could take the role on and make it his own for a new generation. For that reason alone all Bond fans should be very grateful to Sir Roger Moore.

Other Books by John Fox

Timothy Dalton's James Bond - The Retrospective

Timothy Dalton's James Bond - The Retrospective examines the history of Timothy Dalton's relationship with the James Bond franchise from his early days as an actor (amazingly, Dalton was a potential Bond candidate as early as 1968) through to his eventual casting. We'll also take a thorough look at his Bond films from their production to release and see what worked and what didn't. This book will also look at the various doomed plans for a third Timothy Dalton Bond film and examine why Dalton left the role in the end. Most of all, this book is a celebration of Timothy Dalton's James Bond.

No Time to Die - The Unofficial Companion

No Time To Die is destined to be remembered as one of the strangest films in the long history of the legendary James Bond franchise. Not so much for anything in the film or the production (although, as we shall see, the production was far from uneventful and the film's plot may raise a few eyebrows) but because of script and director issues and real world health concerns that have seen the release date for No Time To Die pushed back three times. No Time To Die has been through two massive promotional campaigns, had a Super Bowl spot, released trailers, teasers, promos, a dozen or more posters, featured in numerous magazines and websites, had a podcast, and released a theme song and music video. Bond fans could be forgiven for feeling as if they have been living with No Time To Die for years - only without actually getting to watch the actual film.

No Time to Die - The Unofficial Companion offers a comprehensive and entertaining look at the genesis, production, and seemingly endless release woes of the much anticipated 25th James Bond film.

No Time to Die - The Unofficial Retrospective

My previous book No Time to Die - The Unofficial Companion offered a comprehensive look at the genesis, production, and seemingly endless release woes of the much anticipated 25th James Bond film. Here then is the sequel that everyone asked me to write. No Time to Die - The Unofficial Retrospective covers the final marketing campaign and actual release of No Time to Die and also offers a comprehensive analysis of the film itself, the box-office, fan reaction, the future of the Bond franchise, and much more besides.

www.ingramcontent.com/pod-product-compliance
Lightning Source LLC
Chambersburg PA
CBHW022006120726
47992CB00001B/447